STOCK JALFREZI

A RECIPE FOR SUCCESS IN THE INDIAN STOCK MARKET

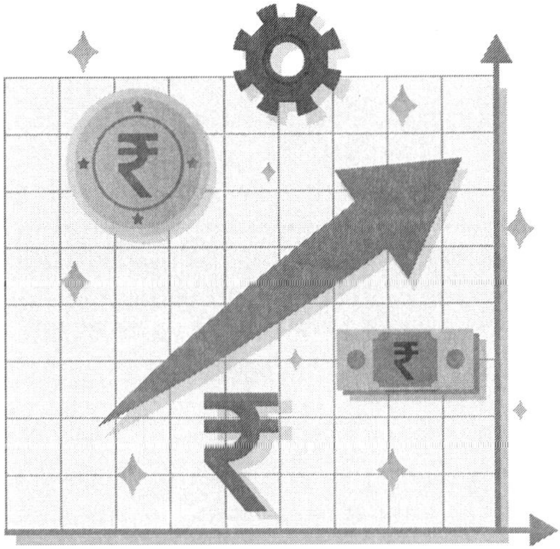

AKASHDEEP GROVER

Clever Fox® PUBLISHING

Chennai • Bangalore

CLEVER FOX PUBLISHING
Chennai, India

Published by CLEVER FOX PUBLISHING 2025

Paperback ISBN: 978-93-6707-969-0
Hardback ISBN: 978-93-6707-061-1

CONTENTS

PREFACE

INDIA'S GOLDEN AGE LIES AHEAD

India stands at a historic turning point, ready to launch like your favourite Diwali rocket. The next 25 years could become India's most exciting era yet, no matter who holds the political remote.

Right now, our economy feels like a Bollywood blockbuster, complete with unexpected twists, high drama, sweeping reforms, tech breakthroughs, and some international masala. But if you look past the theatrics, you'll notice extraordinary opportunities quietly emerging in the stock market.

Today, India is exactly where China stood in the early '90s, on the verge of explosive growth. As we steadily move towards *Viksit Bharat*, market swings will come and go. But investors who stay calm, stick to the fundamentals and maintain a long-term outlook are positioned to reap significant rewards.

India's growth story and your opportunity to benefit from it are just beginning. Play your cards right and your personal golden age may not be far behind.

WHAT IS STOCK JALFREZI?

Stock Jalfrezi is a culmination of insights and lessons from years of navigating the stock market, filled with thrilling wins, painful losses, and invaluable experiences.

Just like the beloved Indian dish *Jalfrezi*, this book blends bold flavours, crunchy insights, generous servings of personal experience, and a pinch of humour. Investing rarely follows a simple recipe. It's more like cooking a *jalfrezi*, packed with bold flavours, unexpected twists, and experiences that challenge, delight, and teach.

I've read several highly acclaimed books by global authors, yet most fail to truly capture the essence of Indian investors. Here, investing is a cultural experience. We have astrology-driven predictions, *chai*-time stock tips, and election-fuelled rallies, i.e., things you won't find in any Wall Street manual. To truly understand Indian markets, you need to understand this chaos. That's exactly why I wrote *Stock Jalfrezi* — to serve up India's stock market madness in a way you can savour.

From spicy market scams to sweet successes, bitter mistakes to tangy wisdom, the book serves up real-life investing stories seasoned with relatable wit. If you've ever fallen for half-baked hot tips or felt lost amid noisy market advice, this book will remind you that successful investing, like great cooking, comes down to knowing your ingredients, trusting your instincts, and always adding a generous dose of common sense.

Inside, you'll find 30 stories, each paired with a practical lesson, delivered with humour and clear analogies designed to stick in your "memeory" (meme + memory, get it?). Forget complicated jargon; investing should feel as comfortable as chatting over *chai* with friends, minus those dubious tips from your neighbourhood uncle's friend's friend.

This book references various stocks, some famous and some infamous, solely to illustrate concepts clearly. They are NOT recommendations or signals to buy or sell. Always do your research, think independently, and invest wisely!

INTRODUCTION

I was introduced to the stock market at the age of 8, all thanks to my elder brother, who was just 13. To be clear, he wasn't an investor, didn't have a demat account, and had absolutely no money in the market. But for some reason, he had this unusual habit of following stock market news over breakfast.

While most kids were watching cartoons or debating whether Maggi should be soupy or dry, our mornings were filled with headlines like *"XYZ stock is up 2% because..."* or *"Sensex crossed 20,000 today"* (which, to my 8-year-old brain, meant someone had just won ₹20,000).

Naturally, I was curious. I started bombarding him with questions like:

"What's Nifty?"

"What's Sensex?"

"Is this real money?"

And like any elder sibling, he answered them with full confidence, whether he knew the answers or not. But I never questioned him. Younger siblings are wired to believe elder siblings always know best.

The best part? He never dismissed my questions. Instead, he encouraged me to follow the markets. That tiny spark lit a fire. Little did he know he was creating a future stock market enthusiast and apparently, an author too.

Fast forward to when I was 19 and doing my CA training. By then, the stock market was no longer just background breakfast chatter, but it was real and I was ready to dive in. Unlike my younger self, who thought the Sensex was some kind of lucky draw, I now had the tools to decode jargon, track trends, and start investing with confidence.

And that's where the journey really began. From a kid asking, *"Is this real money?"* to years of investing, mistakes, wins and lessons, which are enough to fill an entire book. And the learning? It's still going strong.

WHY I WROTE THIS BOOK?

My mission is to help people truly understand investing and personal finance. Let's face it, financial awareness around us is shockingly low. I've seen MBAs, CAs, and even seasoned finance professionals confidently park all their money in fixed deposits and say, *"Stock Market Samajh Nahi Aata"* (I don't understand the stock market). Honestly, that hurts more than a market crash!

I'm here to break this mindset and make investing in stocks as normal as putting money in gold, real estate or fixed deposits. The stock market isn't some get-rich-quick lottery ticket. It's a powerful, legitimate way to steadily build wealth.

Investing in stocks isn't just a passing trend; it's the future. Eventually, you'll join the ride anyway. So why not start now, armed with clarity, confidence, and a head start over unsolicited tips?

MY INVESTMENT PHILOSOPHY

Over the years, I've shaped an investing style that's clear, practical, and built for the long game. It's not about trends, it's about focus. These four principles guide both my investing and this book:

- **Clarity Over Chaos:** If you can't explain why, you own a stock in one line, you probably shouldn't. Every decision I make is grounded in logic, not noise or hype.
- **Think Long, Not Loud:** Markets love drama, but I zoom out, see the bigger picture, and stay focused. Real wealth comes from patience, not reacting to every headline.
- **Keep It Simple:** I like my investing like my writing — clear, direct, and jargon-free. And no, I'm not Ashneer Grover's cousin, but I do share his love for cutting through the nonsense.
- **Emotions on Mute:** Fear, greed, and FOMO should have no place in your decision-making. I rely on fundamentals, stay disciplined, and keep emotions out of the equation.

With that, let's roll up our sleeves, sharpen our instincts, and dive straight into the lessons ahead. The real magic of investing begins now.

SOCH KAR, SAMAJH KAR, INVEST KAR

How much money do you want to make in the next five years?

The question was asked with the seriousness of a typical Bollywood courtroom scene, with an intense death stare and a dramatic pause. On one end of the table, sat Mr. Santosh, the self-proclaimed "King of Good Times" of a company whose business model was as clear as the Delhi winter sky. Around us, *Café Coffee Day* in Connaught Place was buzzing, or as we lovingly call it, "CCD", the unofficial embassy of millennials who ditched *chai* for cold coffee. However, this was not your typical, everyday coffee shop bustle. Here, instead of talking about work or weekend plans, people were gushing over their wealth, luxury cars, and extravagant dreams that seemed straight out of a Karan Johar movie.

Rewind to a few days earlier. I had received a call from Aditya, an old friend whom I admired and held in high esteem. Aditya, a Chartered Accountant fellow and my supervisor during my internship, was known for his sharp judgment and professionalism. When he mentioned a "business opportunity",

I was intrigued. Perhaps, this was my opportunity to escape the predictable life of steady pay checks and delve into the entrepreneurial world I've always dreamed of.

As soon as I stepped into *the café,* I sensed that something was off. The loud discussions about wealth and success created a slightly cult-like atmosphere.

Aditya greeted me warmly and introduced me to a few people... who were quick to share their "success stories". One person had just bought a Mercedes, while another claimed to have earned several lakhs within a few weeks. It was all quite impressive until you realized that their tales of success sounded as if they were scripted by the same writer.

And then came the grand entrance of Mr. Santosh. Dressed in a tailored suit, he exuded authority and his smile communicated, *"Trust me, I know what I'm doing"*. He began with a lecture on financial freedom and then leaned over to me, lowered his voice for effect, and asked: *"How much money do you want to make in the next five years?"*

I decided to play along. *"Five crores"*, I replied, pulling the number out of thin air, much like the claims being made around me. His eyes sparkled; akin to a director who has just found his next lead actor. *"What if I could help you achieve that in just one year?"* he asked, his tone dripping with conviction.

Naturally, I asked the most basic question: *"What is the business model? How does your company make money?"*

What followed was a masterclass in ambiguity. Rather than a clear answer, I received a long-winded monologue about how I could earn my dream car and unimaginable wealth by building my own "downline" (fancy jargon for a pyramid of people who do the hard work while you sit back, count your blessings, and their commissions). The entire scene felt like an episode of *Bigg Boss* — full of drama, yet everyone believed it would culminate in a happy ending with a twist. Spoiler alert! It turned out to be an MLM setup. MLM[1] stands for multi-level marketing, network marketing or, let's call it what it is a *Pyramid scheme*[2]. The name keeps changing, but the story remains the same.

Two hours later, I left the place feeling older, wiser, and considerably more sceptical as Mr. Santosh jumped into an *Uber Pool.* It seemed his dream car was still a work in progress. What should I take from this experience? If someone is selling dreams without substance and clarity, it's time for us to wake up!

MARKET LENS

Much like the MLM schemes I've encountered, there's always someone offering "guaranteed" tips for the next big multi-bagger[3] stock that promises to skyrocket in value within months. You can find these tips in Telegram groups, WhatsApp forwards or even from friends and family.

Here's the hard truth. Don't fall for it if you don't fully understand the business behind the stock. These so-called stock market operators often target low-priced *penny stocks*[4]

---

[1] MLM is a sales strategy where participants earn by selling products and by recruiting others, often structured like a pyramid scheme.

[2] Pyramid scheme is a scam where returns for existing investors are paid from funds contributed by new investors, an unsustainable setup that collapses once recruitment stops.

[3] Multi-bagger is a term for a stock that multiplies in value, giving returns several times the original investment (e.g., a stock that becomes worth 5x or 10x its purchase price).

[4] Penny stocks are very low-priced, small company stock, often highly speculative and illiquid, with high risk of volatility and potential loss.

and create false hype around them. They manipulate prices and temporarily drive them up to attract innocent *"retail investors*[5]*"*. Once enough people have bought in, they sell off their stocks and leave others with worthless stocks. The operators walk away with the profits, while the retail investors are left scratching their heads.

You must have heard phrases like *"something is cooking in this stock"*. But unless you're in the kitchen with the chef, you shouldn't engage in this kind of speculation. These traps are designed to exploit naive investors. Always ask yourself: *"What is this company's business model? How does it make money? Is there something in the financials that justifies the hype?"*

Then there is the infamous "tip aayi hai" brigade. A mysterious stock tip may land in your inbox, promising a hidden gem. But think for a moment. Why are you getting this tip and why is it free? As the saying goes, *"There's no such thing as a free lunch"*. If someone offers you a hot stock tip, there's a good chance you're being used to keep the scam going. Free tips are often used to manipulate stock prices and take advantage of retail investors.

I recommend taking the so-called "credibility test". Ask yourself: *"Is the person offering this tip truly credible when it comes to stock recommendations?"* If the answer is NO, it's best to steer clear.

And then there are the self-proclaimed "market experts" you see on TV. Every morning, they come on with a new list of stocks you should buy or sell. But here's the thing, they're not responsible for any losses you incur based on their tips. Their

---

[5] Retail investors are individual (non-professional) investor who buys and sells securities for their personal account, as opposed to large institutional investors.

main objective is to boost ratings (TRP), not necessarily to help you grow your wealth. It's crucial to filter out the noise. Furthermore, check these so-called experts for credibility. Are they answerable if their tips fail?

Ask questions, seek clarity, and make sure you understand the business before you invest. That's the heart of the **S.A.M.J.H.O.** strategy and your shortcut to making smarter, well-informed decisions.

S - SOURCE OF REVENUE

Ask: How does the company make money?

Why: If you don't know where the money comes from, you're flying blind.

A - ASSETS AND LIABILITIES

Ask: What does the company own and how much debt does it have?

Why: A strong financial foundation means that the company can weather storms without sinking.

M - MANAGEMENT MATTERS

Ask: Who runs the company? Do they have a good track record?

Why: Trustworthy and capable leaders drive success.

J - JOURNEY AHEAD

Ask: What is the company's growth potential?

Why: Yesterday's stars are no guarantee of tomorrow's blockbusters; always look ahead.

H - HEALTH OF FINANCIALS

Ask: Are profits constant and are revenues growing?

Why: A company with shaky finances is like a house of cards. One strong gust of wind and everything collapses.

O - OWNERSHIP STRUCTURE

Ask: Who owns the company and are their interests aligned with yours?

Why: If the promoters are not backing their own business, why should you?

The S.A.M.J.H.O. strategy may not answer all your questions, but it will give you the basics to make smarter and more informed decisions. Just like "PK" from the Amir Khan movie, who questioned everything around him, you need to adopt the same inquisitive, exploratory mindset when it comes to your investments. In finance, this principle is like *"KYC: Know Your Customer[6]"*. When investing, you should adhere to "Know Your Stock", meaning you should understand a

---

[6] KYC are regulations requiring institutions to verify the identity and background of clients to prevent fraud and money laundering.

company's financials, business model, and growth potential before investing your hard-earned money in it.

> **Quick Hack**
>
> **Follow the 30-second rule:** If you can't explain how a company makes money in 30 seconds, that's a warning signal. That's your signal to walk away and avoid speculation.

FROM MY JOURNEY

I'd be lying if I said I wasn't tempted by the market glitter. I remember back in 2015 when I first ventured into the stock market with my precious stipend. Back then, Dr. Datson Labs was the stock everyone was talking about. Funnily enough, I never bothered to look at the numbers of this company, even though, as a CA student, I was knee-deep in the financial reports that were just a click away on the NSE[7] or BSE[8] website. Instead, like an extra in a Bollywood movie enjoying the dance without knowing the plot, I got carried away by the hype and rode the wave without questioning the business model or the financials.

Then, on May 22, 2015, reality hit me. I learned that trading for Dr. Datson Labs had been suspended on both exchanges

[7] NSE (National Stock Exchange) is one of the major stock exchanges in India, where stocks and other securities are traded.

[8] BSE (Bombay Stock Exchange) is Asia's oldest stock exchange, based in Mumbai, India; a major marketplace for trading stocks.

because the promoters had pledged[9] their entire shareholdings, which were then claimed by the lenders. Boom! Just like that, my entire investment in that stock vanished into thin air.

I wrote the same lesson in *My Investment Diary.* Ah, the legendary investment diary! A treasure chest of lessons learned and wisdom gained. It's like a scrapbook of my financial journey, but instead of glitter and stickers, it's full of market insights and "aha" moments. Think of it as my personal "back to the future" investing time machine. Here is a nugget from *My Investment Diary,* dated May 22, 2015:

My Investment Diary

Today, I learned a hard lesson. I lost my entire investment in Dr. Datson Labs after trading in the company's stocks was suspended on the NSE and BSE. The promoters had pledged all their stocks and the lenders took control. I should have done more research on the business and the company's financial situation before investing.

This experience made me realize the importance of analyzing a company's fundamentals when picking the right stock.

Debit: "Losses incurred on Dr. Datson Labs stock"
Credit: "Priceless lesson on the importance of research and analysis"
(Net balance: A modest, wise and research-oriented investor)

22 May 2015
(Friday)

[9] Pledged stocks are the stocks that have been used as collateral for a loan. Promoters may "pledge" their stock holdings to borrow money; if they can't repay, lenders can sell these shares, potentially harming the stock price.

The money is gone and so is the time, but it's still in my portfolio today. Not as a valuable asset, but as a priceless reminder of my early investing innocence. It's like having an Oscar-worthy drama in my portfolio, a reminder of a lesson worth many crores. Here's a snapshot of Dr Datson Labs transaction from my demat account:

Snapshot From My Investment Account

Name	Qty Long Term Qty	LTP	Avg Price	Inv Val	Cur Val	P&L
DR. DATSONS LABS LTD	730.00	6.40	13.67	9,979.10	4,672.00	-5,307.10 (-53.18%)

Today, the market is full of what I call "hot air balloon stocks" These are stocks based on nothing but hype. A closer look often reveals that many of them belong to a particular group of companies in India that has close ties to powerful people. Even though I don't mention the names (because my peace of mind is priceless), these stocks often go up because of their influence and not their performance. That's why I stay away from them and recommend you do the same. Don't buy dreams, invest in what you really understand.

THE BOTTOM LINE

The conclusion here? Soch Kar, Samajh Kar, Invest Kar. Don't invest just because your friend's uncle said he got a "hot tip". Ask questions, understand the business, and know its fundamentals. Channel your inner PK. Be inquisitive and don't settle for vague answers. In the stock market, "Know

Your Stocks" is your version of KYC. Don't buy into dreams; invest in what's real.

As the saying goes, *"Fortune favours the prepared mind"*. Or as I see it, *"The prepared investor finds the real treasure"*.

The man who asks a question is a fool for a minute, the man who does not ask is a fool for life.

- Confucius
(Chinese philosopher)

BHAV BHAGWAN CHHE

Have you ever paid for something and later wondered if you bought the product or the hype?

A vegetable market is like a comedy stage. Full of drama, suspense, and priceless one-liners. Just the other day, I visited and walked through such a market to buy potatoes. At the first stall, I came across a mountain of mud-kissed potatoes costing ₹10 per kg. My first thought? No way! I mean these potatoes looked like they had just come back from a wrestling match with the mud. Feeling unimpressed, I moved on.

Then, I discovered the real gems. Potatoes that could pass off as jewellery. These beauties were golden, shiny, and practically screamed, *"Put me on Instagram!"* I was hooked. Whether it was a secret polishing technique, or they were simply *born to shine*, these spuds looked like they were ready for a debut at McDonald's. When I asked the seller for the price, expecting maybe ₹30 or ₹40 per kilo, I was shocked! ₹150 per kilo. Half-laughing and half-choking, I asked, *"For the whole truck?"* The vendor smiled and said, *"Sir, no more dad jokes"*. Thanks to the transport strike, prices were as inflated as my dreams of early retirement.

At that moment, clarity struck me like a bolt of lightning. I had dismissed those dirty ₹10 potatoes before. Suddenly they looked like hidden gems waiting to be discovered. I thought about it again. After all, with a quick rinse and a scrubbing brush, the cheaper potatoes could be used quite well for *Dum Aloo.* Let's face it, whether you're frying them or baking them, potatoes aren't exactly a healthy food, so why spend money on fancy ones? It's not about their shine; it's about their value. A lesson straight out of *Spudonomics 101!* And isn't that the golden rule of investing, too? Price isn't just a number; it's the silent dealmaker or deal-breaker.

MARKET LENS

A stock can be incredibly attractive in terms of growth and market positioning, but the price you pay for that potential can make the difference between success and failure. Just like in the vegetable market, in the stock market, too *Bhav Bhagwan Chhe* or Valuation is King.

The potato drama may tickle your funny bone, but the lesson it teaches is no joke, especially in the world of investing. In the stock market, every price tag tells a story and the key is knowing whether it's a masterpiece or a poorly written script.

Let me give you an example. Imagine two companies:

(1) Company ABC, the darling of the financial news and the star of every analyst's report. ABC boasts an expected sales growth of 50% and a hefty 40% profit margin.
(2) Company XYZ, the underdog that everyone overlooks. XYZ bumbles along with just 5% growth and a razor-thin 5% profit margin.

On the surface, ABC looks like a dream stock — fast-growing, popular, and the stuff of portfolio fantasies. XYZ, on the other hand, is the dusty potato sitting at the back of the stall. It doesn't make the headlines and honestly, nobody discusses it over coffee.

If you had to decide based solely on the information available, Company ABC would be the obvious choice, wouldn't it? You might already be imagining the growth curve, juicy dividends, and maybe even the yacht you'll buy with your profits.

But wait; you're in for a surprise! ABC's stock trades at a *Price-to-Earnings (P/E)*[10] ratio of 100, while XYZ's stock trades at a P/E ratio of just 10. With such a high valuation, any good news for ABC is already priced in. One misstep and the market romance could crash harder than a Bollywood box-office flop. On the other hand, XYZ's modest P/E ratio of 10 seems more like a diamond in the rough, allowing room for surprises. A new product launch or a surge in demand could double or even triple XYZ's value turning the company into an unexpected blockbuster that no one saw coming.

This is where valuation works its magic. Prices aren't just numbers; they reflect the market's expectations of the future. If those expectations are already sky-high, your upside is as limited as the chance of finding a parking spot in Mumbai during rush hour. When prices are low and expectations are modest, even small improvements can lead to substantial

---

[10] P/E ratio is a valuation metric showing how much investors are paying for each unit of a company's earnings. Calculated as market price per share divided by earnings per share (EPS). EPS is a company's profit divided by the number of outstanding shares. Indicates how much profit is attributable to each share of stock.

gains. It's not just about finding a great stock; it's about finding a great stock at the right price.

Now that we understand the problem, let's talk about solutions. What should you do? If you come across a stock that seems too tempting to resist, hold your horses! There's a simple litmus test called PEG (and no, it's not our beloved *Punjabi peg!*). PEG[11] stands for *Price-to-Earnings-to-Growth.* An important metric that helps you decide whether a stock is really worth its value. Here's how it works:

[11] PEG ratio is defined as P/E ratio divided by the company's earnings growth rate. Helps evaluate if a high P/E is justified by growth; for example, a PEG above 1 may indicate an overvalued stock.

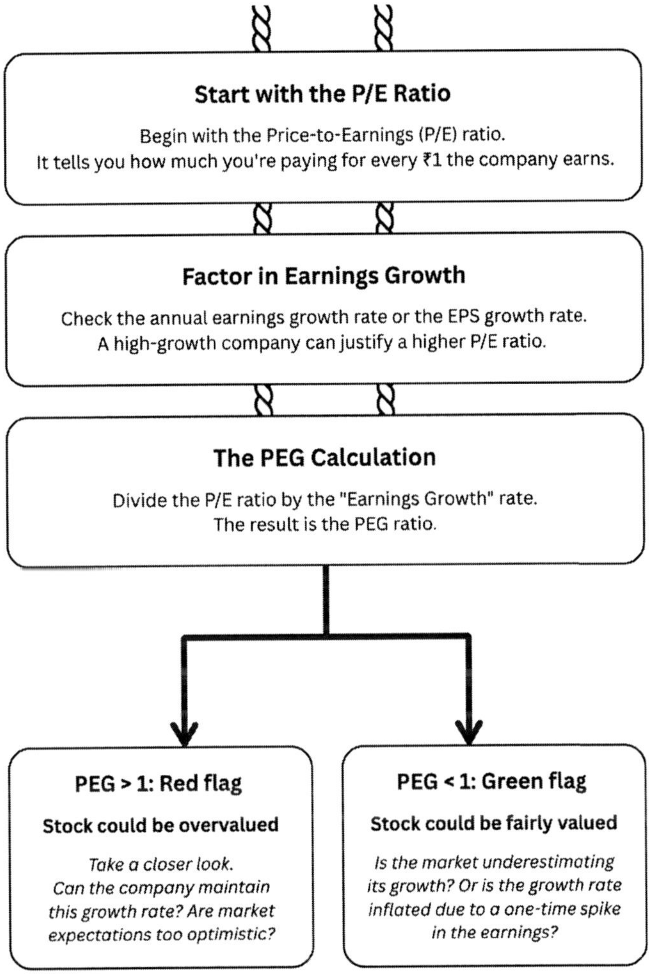

Of course, the PEG ratio isn't the ultimate answer to all your investment questions, but it's a litmus test for first impressions. The PEG ratio can provide a reasonable indication of whether the company's growth is realistic or merely hype. It acts as a shortcut to identify overvalued stocks and protect your portfolio from overpriced traps. In short, don't be blinded by shiny valuations. If the price tag screams luxury, ensure it's backed by performance.

FROM MY JOURNEY

In my journey as an investor, I've come across both shiny and muddy potatoes in abundance. One of the first lessons I learned was not to get swept by the hype around growth stocks.

It's 2021 and Clean Science & Technology's IPO[12] is the talk of the town. A juggernaut in specialty chemicals with a balance sheet as strong as Arnold Schwarzenegger (or as some Delhiites say, Arnold SubhashNagar because who has time for tricky pronunciations?). The growth rates were mind-boggling and profit margins were simply enviable. It was the Bollywood blockbuster of IPOs! Everyone I knew was queuing up to buy stocks, convinced it was going to skyrocket.

I must admit I was tempted as well. However, there was a catch: valuation. The stock was trading at a sky-high 100x P/E upon its listing (around ₹1,700). That's like paying five-star prices for a *Dhaba meal!* It may be delicious, but is it really worth the cost? My instinct said no. Instead of jumping in headfirst, I put the stock on my watch list and waited for a correction.

Meanwhile, my friends and colleagues happily jumped on the bandwagon as the stock rose to over ₹2,500 within a few months, fuelled by the market euphoria. The dreaded

---

[12] IPO is the first sale of a company's shares to the public via a stock exchange, transitioning the company from private to publicly traded.

FOMO (Fear of Missing Out)[13] crept in. *"What if I'm wrong?"* I wondered. Yet, I adhered to my analysis and didn't succumb to the hype, because sometimes patience isn't just a virtue; it's the best investment strategy!

Like a twist in a Bollywood movie, reality made its grand entrance months later. The stock price crashed. My friends, who had been enjoying their quick gains, were now left empty-handed as their profits had disappeared.

As of December 2024, the stock price hovered around ₹1,300, still below its listing value, even though the company's revenues and profits have increased since 2021. Why was there such drama? Because *Bhav Bhagwan Chhe!* The high valuation at that point had already priced in years of growth, leaving little room for upside. Here is a golden nugget from *My Investment Diary* dated August 4, 2023:

[13] FOMO is a common investor emotion – the anxiety of missing a potential profit – often leading to impulsive buying of popular stocks simply because others are doing so.

My Investment Diary

Today, my decision to avoid Clean Science stocks has paid off. The stock, which reached ₹2,500+ in 2021, has now fallen to ₹1,309.

This experience has taught me two important lessons: valuation matters, and if you stay disciplined, you can avoid falling for market hype.

Debit: "A lifelong lesson on the power of valuation"
Credit: "Money saved by avoiding the overpriced hype surrounding Clean Science"
(Net balance: A smarter, value-oriented investor with unwavering patience)

04 Aug 2023
(Friday)

On the other hand, I also experienced success with stocks that nobody seemed to notice. Take Marksans Pharma, for example. Back in 2022, the stock price was around ₹60, which is like a hidden jewel at the bottom of a treasure chest. I saw the solid fundamentals and knew there was gold beneath the surface. Within a few years: boom! The value of the stock quadrupled (4x). What we call in Punjabi *"balle balle"* returns. What was my secret here? It was not only about recognizing potential but about seizing it at the right price.

Quick Hack

Track your favourite stocks using price alerts in apps. Wait for a correction before you jump in because buying at the right price can dramatically increase your long-term returns.

THE BOTTOM LINE

These experiences taught me an invaluable lesson. Price is just as important as quality. Buying a top-tier company at an inflated price is like being late for the all-you-can-eat buffet — disappointing and not worth it!

In this stock market game, patience and discipline are your trusty allies and they have often led me to victory. As the legendary Charlie Munger once said: *"The big money is not in buying and selling but in the waiting"*.

The price you pay today determines the performance of your portfolio tomorrow. If you make the right choices, you'll see your wealth grow steadily. However, if you make the wrong decisions, you may find yourself sidelined, watching others enjoy gains while you experience regret.

Whether you're haggling over *Bhindi* or analysing stock charts, one rule always applies: Valuation is King! The most glamorous stock isn't always the best deal if the price is too high. Sometimes, the overlooked, dusty underdog, the undervalued stocks, have the greatest potential for growth. So, the next time you're tempted by a high-flying stock, pause, and ask yourself: "*How high is its valuation and does it make sense?*"

Remember, the stock market ultimately follows the same principles as life itself – *Bhav Bhagwan Chhe!*

Not everything is as it seems, and not everything that seems is.

- Albert Einstein
(German theoretical physicist)

3

THE 'GOLMAAL' THEORY

Have you ever walked into an offer so tempting that saying 'no' felt like a crime?

Let me share a story about my wife and I moving back to Gurgaon in 2023. A city where every second advertisement promises a luxury experience, every third person claims to be a real estate expert, and every fourth scheme is *too good to be true*.

One evening, we received an invitation for a luxury club membership event at a five-star hotel. We weren't exactly planning to sign up, but free coffee and cookies at a luxury hotel? Why not! As self-proclaimed explorers (or, to be honest, just two curious people who like to get something for free), we decided to give it a try.

So, we found ourselves in the basement of this five-star hotel. Yes, you read that right — Basement. The atmosphere felt less like luxurious hospitality and more like the set of a low-budget news show exposing scams. Banners with the words "Taj Hospitality" hung on the walls, which looked impressive at first glance, but something felt off upon closer inspection.

Then came Mr. V, an overly enthusiastic salesman brimming with confidence like a Shark Tank judge we never asked for. He launched into a detailed presentation:

"Just a one-time payment and unlimited stays at our partner resorts!"

"Exclusive membership with 80% discount; but only if you sign up NOW!"

"Oh, and scratch cards, free stays, lucky draws! Win a free trip to the Maldives!"

I have a simple rule. Never make financial decisions in the heat of the moment. But Mr. V was relentless and did not take the easy way out. Putting in more effort than a fitness trainer during the New Year rush. He made us feel foolish for even considering turning down this once-in-a-lifetime offer.

But the biggest red flag? No mobile network. Since we were in the basement, a quick Google search to check the legitimacy of the company was out of the question. Coincidence? I doubt it. So, I excused myself to the upstairs washroom, where I finally got some signal and did a quick search.

Bingo! The reviews were a horror show.

Fraudulent complaints, misleading plans, unfulfilled promises it was all there. When I returned, I noticed them giving out "achievement awards" to people who made instant purchases. Who were these people? Real buyers? Paid actors? Innocent victims? Who knows!

My wife and I simply smiled, enjoyed our free cookies and walked out. Mr. V's face darkened as he realized that he had lost two potential customers who would not fall for the trap.

As we left the hotel, I laughed and said, *"Golmaal hai bhai, sab Golmaal hai"*. Little did I know that this experience was the perfect metaphor for how things work in the stock market.

MARKET LENS

The stock market isn't so different from my experience in the five-star basement. Every now and then, you'll come across a stock that seems like a once-in-a-lifetime opportunity that you can't afford to miss. You hear self-proclaimed stock market gurus, WhatsApp stock tipsters and financial influencers (who only discovered investing last week) scream:

"This stock is the next HDFC Bank!"

"10x returns guaranteed! Just look at the last 6 months!"

"Even FIIs[14] *are investing heavily! Don't miss out!"*

Sounds tempting, right? Just like my free five-star "luxury" membership. But here's the thing. These sensationalised claims often manipulate investor sentiment and create FOMO (Fear of Missing Out).

If you think that's just theory, let's talk about the recent stock market scam in Assam, one of the most recent and blatant examples of how hype-driven scams work.

A group of scammers in Assam lured investors with promises of guaranteed returns of 30% in just 60 days; an offer so enticing it seemed almost magical. To appear legitimate, they even issued written agreements on stamp paper, giving victims a false sense of security.

---

[14] FIIs are institutional investor from outside the country who invests in the country's financial markets (for example, a foreign mutual fund or pension fund investing in Indian stocks).

The result? A staggering ₹2,200 crore vanished, fuelling the fraudsters' extravagant lifestyles. They invested in luxury properties, luxury cars, and even an Assamese cinema; all to create an illusion of success and attract more victims. It was the same old scam in a new guise with unrealistic promises, ostentatious wealth, and fake guarantees, all carefully crafted to deceive unsuspecting investors.

It's not much different in the stock market. Very often, you hear about a penny stock that's "guaranteed" to skyrocket, or a *Mutual Fund*[15] that will make you rich overnight. But ask yourself, if the offer is so great, why is it advertised so aggressively? Why the urgency?

If you think investors only fall for *Ponzi schemes*[16], you're mistaken. Sometimes, all it takes is a misleading name. During the COVID-19 crisis in India, when the country faced a severe oxygen shortage, investors rushed into oxygen manufacturing stocks. Amidst this frenzy, the stocks of Bombay Oxygen Investments skyrocketed, driven by its exposure to oxygen supply. The catch? The company hadn't been in the oxygen business for years; it had transitioned into a non-banking financial company (NBFC) that had nothing to do with oxygen production. Nevertheless, driven by name confusion and sheer panic, investors pounced on the company.

This fiasco is reminiscent of "Golmaal". Just because a company's name sounds relevant doesn't mean its business is.

---

[15] Mutual Funds are investment vehicle pooling money from many investors to buy a diversified portfolio of stocks, bonds, or other assets.

[16] Ponzi scheme is a fraudulent investment scheme where returns to earlier investors are paid from the contributions of newer investors, rather than actual profits. Such schemes collapse when new money stops coming in.

So before chasing hot tips, ask yourself: *"Am I investing in a solid business or just a catchy name?"*

Now that you've learned how to recognise the red flags and avoid falling for a "Golmaal" scam, what should you do instead? Here's a quick checklist to keep you on the right track:

✦ **Do Your Homework**

Conduct thorough research before you invest. Check the fundamentals of the company, i.e., Balance sheets, quality of management, and its reputation in the market. If a company refuses to answer basic questions or only provides vague information about its activities, you should steer clear.

✦ **Question the Urgency**

Beware of exaggerated sales tactics. *"Invest now or miss out forever!"* With serious offers, you don't have to make quick decisions.

✦ **Look for Transparency**

Look out for companies that openly report on their performance, strategies, and risks. Regular information for investors, earnings announcements, and clear financial reports indicate good *corporate governance*[17].

✦ **Avoid Guaranteed Returns**

In the real world, no one can promise steady double-digit profits without risk. If someone claims that there is *no risk*, it is probably too good to be true.

[17] Corporate governance is the system of rules, practices, and processes by which a company is directed and controlled. Good corporate governance (transparent management, accountability to shareholders, etc.) signals a well-run, accountable company.

✦ Verify Credentials

Whether it's a stock tip from a self-proclaimed guru or a friend, always do your research. A simple online check for reviews, regulatory warnings or previous complaints can save you from making a costly mistake.

✦ Seek Professional Advice

If you have any doubts, contact a certified *financial planner*[18] or a trusted advisor. A real advisor won't push you into risky deals for a quick commission.

Genuine investment opportunities don't need to come with bells, whistles, and flashing neon signs. If someone bombards you with vouchers, scratchcards, and instant bonuses, it's not an investment opportunity; it's a red flag, just like the flashy "Taj Hospitality" deal.

Good investments are simple. If you stick to transparent, fundamentally strong stocks, you will always do better in the long run than these too-good-to-be-true schemes.

Did You Know ?

SEBI clearly restricts anyone (including advisors) from claiming guarantees for assured returns in the stock market.

[18] Financial Planner is a professional who helps individuals manage their finances, including investments, retirement planning, tax strategies, and wealth management.

FROM MY JOURNEY

I wasn't always this cautious. A few years ago, I was lured into an "exclusive, high-return, no-risk" programme by a good friend; someone I trusted enough to lend my phone when it had only 10% battery left, no questions asked. The sales pitch was irresistible: *"Invest once, get weekly payouts, and double your money in two years!"*

For the first six months, life felt like a carnival of money printing. Every week, there was a nice little deposit into my account. I envisioned retiring early and maybe even opening a beach *café* in Goa or buying a fully loaded SUV. The plan felt foolproof. I was already drafting a blog post titled *"How I cracked the stock market code"*.

But then came the turning point which felt more like a balloon bursting at a child's birthday party. After six months, the weekly payouts stopped. Poof. Disappeared. Completely. The company vanished faster than my no-carb promise at an all-you-can-eat buffet. Overnight, hundreds of us were left high and dry, frantically texting, and emailing a company that no longer existed. It turned out that our "returns" had been paid out of newer investors' money (a classic Ponzi scheme) and when the inflow dried up, the entire facade collapsed like a poorly built house of cards. In the end, we lost our hard-earned savings. My initial visions of being a "financial genius" were replaced by a queasy feeling that screamed, *"Golmaal hai bhai, sab Golmaal hai!"*. I have documented the lesson in *My Investment Diary*. Here is the excerpt:

My Investment Diary

Today, I learned the hard way that there is no such thing as "zero risk". The weekly payouts were stopped and the company disappeared into thin air and so did my savings.

This experience taught me a simple but important lesson: if something sounds too good to be true, it's probably a trap.

Debit: "Hard-earned money lost through a Ponzi scheme"
Credit: "A valuable lesson on how quickly 'Golmaal' can happen"
(Net balance: A more cautious investor who will never again fall for "guaranteed" programmes)

12 Dec 2018
(Wednesday)

That was my rude awakening. There are no magic formulas for instant wealth. If something promises incredible returns without risk, then it is surely more fantasy than finance. Every time I encounter an investment that sounds too perfect, I think back to the six glorious months of "easy money" that quickly turned into a nightmare. My golden rule now? If it seems too good to be true, it's probably a setup for your downfall.

THE BOTTOM LINE

When it comes to investing, remember the simple mantra — *"Golmaal hai bhai, sab Golmaal hai!"* i.e., if something seems too flashy, too pushy or too perfect, it's probably just a trap.

Just like the "luxury" seminar in the basement or a Ponzi scheme that pays off until it collapses, these "sure shot" offers lure you in with the promise of quick profits and zero risk.

In the real world, successful investing is not about seeking shortcuts or succumbing to urgent offers; it's about patience, research, and rational decision-making. If a company, or a so-called "expert" is relying on high-pressure tactics, excessive incentives or guaranteed returns, you should take a step back. Good opportunities don't need to scream for attention; they demonstrate their value through solid fundamentals, transparency, and long-term potential.

So, the next time you come across an unbeatable offer, ask yourself, *"Does this sound like a plot twist from a Golmaal movie?"* If it does, treat it like a comedy — enjoy the show, have a laugh, but don't buy a ticket. Stick to serious investments, stay alert for red flags and always do your homework. Because in the stock market, the best strategy is usually the one that is free of unnecessary drama.

It is easier to fool people than to convince them that they have been fooled.

- Mark Twain
(American writer and humourist)

SUCCESS STARTS WITH 'NO'

What would you do if your greatest success turned into your greatest dilemma?

It was the day I received my 10th-grade results. Although I was never the class topper, I had always been a good student. My parents always stressed the importance of the 10th-grade marksheet, seeing it as not only proof of academic achievement but also evidence of my age, which I later realised is oddly common in small towns. Needless to say, I was nervous.

When the results were announced, I was stunned. Not only had I topped my school, but the whole town! My parents were overjoyed, my relatives came to congratulate me and for a moment, I felt like a Bollywood hero basking in the glory of a blockbuster success. But then came the question that cut through my euphoria like a twist in a suspenseful thriller, *"What subjects are you going to choose next?"*

Friends, relatives, and neighbours all joined in, echoing the same question: *"What's next? What's next?"*. It felt like the legendary scene in Baahubali movie, where a single cry of *"Baahubali!"* triggers a roaring chorus among the crowd. My joy turned to confusion and that moment of glory suddenly felt like a growing pressure that I wasn't prepared for.

I went to one of my teachers in the hope that he would help me. He listened patiently as I expressed my insecurities, then asked me the same dreaded question, *"What do you want to do?"*

For the first time, I blurted out, *"I don't know what I want to do, but I know what I don't want to do. I don't want to study medicine or engineering; I'm scared of Physics, Chemistry, and Biology!"*

I had expected him to be disappointed. Instead, he smiled and said something that has stayed with me to this day: *"Knowing what you don't want to do is also a decision"*. That was my eureka moment. By ruling out what I didn't want, I found the clarity to pursue commerce. That choice eventually made me a CA and a CFA charterholder and shaped my entire career journey.

The lesson that day was crystal clear. Discovering what to avoid is just as important, and sometimes even more so, than figuring out what to pursue. In fact, it often serves as the first real step in making any meaningful decision.

MARKET LENS

The stock market is no different, with over 5,000 stocks on the BSE and more than 2,000 on the NSE, it often feels like looking for a needle in a haystack. However, there's good news. Knowing which stocks to avoid can make the process much easier.

Over the years, I have developed a series of *"don'ts"*. These are simple rules that have saved me from countless poor investment decisions. And to keep things engaging, I share these rules with a dash of fun analogies to make them easy to understand and hard to forget:

- **Governance problems:** If management or auditors resign citing governance issues, that's a major red flag. Imagine the captain of the Titanic abandoning the ship; this stock is heading straight for an iceberg. Don't wait to find out how cold the water is; jump before it sinks.
- **Low trading volume:** Stocks with low trading volume are like the deserted village in *Sholay*— no buyers, no liquidity[19], only the echo of Gabbar's laugh somewhere in the distance. SEBI[20] even classifies such securities as "illiquid" based on their trading frequency and volume. Investing in such stocks can be risky, if you try to sell, you could find yourself trapped with Gabbar Singh, i.e., with a bad investment and no way out.
- **Declining promoter participation:** When promoters start selling their stocks, it's like a star soccer player moving to another team just before the crucial final match. If they don't have confidence in the club (or the company), why should you?
- **Pending legal proceedings:** Legal troubles can cripple a business and strain its finances. It's like booking a house involved in a real estate dispute, i.e., you could spend years

[19] Liquidity is the ease with which an asset (like a stock) can be bought or sold at stable prices. A liquid stock has plenty of buyers and sellers (easy to trade); an illiquid stock is hard to sell quickly without significantly affecting the price.

[20] SEBI (Securities and Exchange Board of India) is the regulatory authority for the securities markets in India. SEBI oversees and regulates stock exchanges and market participants and works to protect investor interests.

in court, caught up in drama, with no resolution in sight while your money hangs in the balance.

- **Transactions with related parties:** Excessive transactions with related parties often indicate the misappropriation of funds. These involve dealings between the company and entities connected to the promoters or management such as family, friends or other businesses they own. Imagine Suresh Bakery buying all its ingredients from Uncle Ramesh's overpriced grocery store. Not only are you overpaying, but you are also unknowingly funding the family drama.
- **High debt ratios:** Companies drowning in debt during a downturn are like marathon runners carrying a 50-pound backpack; they'll collapse before reaching the finish line and so will your investment. To identify a debt-heavy company, there's a quick rule of thumb — *Debt-to-equity (D/E)*[21] *ratio.* If it's over 1.5 to 2 times, that's a warning sign, though this also varies by industry.
- **Poor disclosure practices:** Companies that fail to disclose important information are a disaster waiting to happen. Poor disclosure means irregular reporting, frequent revisions or restatements, incomplete details, or reluctance to address important issues in earnings releases. It's like watching a Christopher Nolan's movie without subtitles (you know, the guy behind *Inception* movie, who made us question reality), you're left in the dark and confusion is guaranteed.
- **Involvement in scandal:** A company entangled in a scandal or fraud is like the movie *Race*. Everyone's playing dirty and

[21] Debt-to-Equity ratio is a financial ratio that compares a company's total debt to its shareholders' equity. It indicates the level of financial leverage a company is using.

you could end up with nothing. Even if the company tries to make amends, the risk usually isn't worth it.

- **Accusations of insider trading:** When insiders prioritize their own pockets over those of shareholders, it's a recipe for disaster. It's like imagining a version of *Sholay* where Jai is secretly working for Gabbar. Betrayal is inevitable and the consequences won't be pretty.

These aren't rigid rules, but practical guidelines that can help you avoid costly mistakes. The next time you're tempted to invest in a stock that seems too good to be true, stop, and ask yourself: *"Does it break any of these rules?"* If the answer is yes, it's best to steer clear. Remember in the long run, knowing what to avoid is just as important, if not more than finding the next big winner.

FROM MY JOURNEY

I want to take you to a moment that changed my perspective on investing; a stock forever etched in my memory, known as Dena Bank.

Dena Bank was a name synonymous with history and heritage, but it was also tainted with bad loans and a weak financial position. Despite my usual scepticism about highly regulated companies, I was lured to Dena Bank by expert opinions, hoping for a Bollywood-worthy plot twist.

However, when the RBI placed the bank under Prompt Corrective Action (PCA), the writing was on the wall. For those unfamiliar, PCA is like RBI putting the bank in ICU. This includes severe restrictions, such as limiting lending, which is vital for any bank's survival. Without new loans, growth stalls, and the path to recovery disappears. Despite this, many investors, including myself, held on to the hope of an epic comeback. *Spoiler alert: no miracles.*

In 2018, the Indian government announced the merger of Dena Bank with Bank of Baroda and Vijaya Bank as part of its strategy to consolidate public sector banks. While some mergers can feel like exciting surprises, this was not one of those cases. For Dena Bank shareholders like me, it felt more like being left at the altar. The stocks were delisted and the terms of the merger resulted in losses for most investors.

No amount of faith or hope could rewrite this script, the government's decision was final. Here's a little look into the past. A snapshot of Dena Bank's stock price from 2013 until its unfortunate exit from the market.

Dena Bank Stock Price Chart (2013–2019)

For me, this was a wake-up call; a loud and clear reminder that the influence of regulators, especially in sectors controlled by the government, is a bright red flag. Here's a golden nugget from *My Investment Diary:*

My Investment Diary

Today, I faced a harsh reality with the delisting of Dena Bank. Due to an unfavourable exchange ratio in the merger, I received only 110 stocks of Bank of Baroda for my 1,000 stocks of Dena Bank which were far less than I had expected. Following the announcement, the stock price has declined, and now I wish I had trusted my instincts earlier.

Debit: "Losses from the stocks of Dena Bank"
Credit: "An important lesson in recognising red flags and understanding the risks of regulatory action"
(Net balance: A cautious investor now better able to spot danger signs)

07 Mar 2019
(Thursday)

However, the lesson was not over yet. Many of my friends succumbed to the lure of "cheap" *PSU*[22] *stocks* like IDBI Bank and MTNL, believing they had discovered hidden treasures. Unfortunately, they learned the hard way that "cheap" does not always mean "valuable". Most of them saw their investments plummet, which reinforced my belief that knowing "what to avoid" in the stock market is just as important as finding the next big winner.

This experience served not just as a reminder, but a mantra. Don't chase the hype, steer clear of traps, and always say no to stocks waving red flags.

[22] Public Sector Undertakin is defined as a company with a majority ownership by the government.

Pro Tip

Say NO before you say YES: When selecting a stock, filter out those that violate your key investment principles. Removing weak contenders early helps you focus on right opportunities for better investment decisions.

THE BOTTOM LINE

When it comes to investing, we all dream of finding the next big multi-bagger, the stock that will elevate us from zero to hero.

Benjamin Graham, the father of value investing, put it in a nutshell when he said: *"The essence of investment management is the management of risks, not the management of returns"*. What does this mean? Avoiding bad investments acts as a safety net for your financial goals. It doesn't guarantee you won't experience setbacks, but it cushions the blow and protects your hard-earned capital.

Chasing gains is exciting, but avoiding losses is the smarter strategy. Stick to your investment strategy, embrace your lessons, and remember that knowing what not to do is often your greatest superpower in the stock market.

The art of being wise is knowing what to overlook.

- William James
(American philosopher)

WHAT MATTERS 'MOAT'

Would you rather have an army of a thousand soldiers or an unarmed strategist who can outsmart any opponent?

For Arjun in the *Mahabharata,* the answer was crystal clear. He chose strategy over strength. When Shri Krishna offered him a choice between his powerful army and the unarmed Shri Krishna himself, Arjun chose him. Duryodhan, his rival, couldn't believe his luck; he eagerly grabbed the army and probably thought, *"more soldiers, more power!"*

However, history shows, Arjun's decision led to victory. Shri Krishna's wisdom, strategic insight, and unparalleled ability to think several steps ahead were worth more than a thousand armies combined. It wasn't about sheer numbers, but rather about having an unbeatable advantage.

This timeless epic serves as a perfect metaphor for understanding moats in business. In the business world, *moat*[23] symbolises a company's enduring edge over its rivals. It isn't merely about having a big team or fancy resources; it's about possessing

---

[23] Moat is a term used to describe a company's sustainable competitive advantage that protects it from competitors.

something unique and irreplaceable. An advantage that no competitor can replicate.

Take Amul, the desi OG champion of the dairy industry in India. If you think Amul's success is all about butter and cheese, you've only skimmed the surface (pun intended). *Hold on to my lassi!* The real secret lies in the robust cooperative model. Amul has empowered rural farmers not just as suppliers but as stakeholders. This unwavering loyalty, combined with a seamless supply chain, has created a divide that competitors cannot bridge. While competitors may attempt to spread their wings, Amul remains rich and creamy, benefitting from a full-fat advantage. You can compete on price, product or marketing, but Amul has an army of loyal farmers who consistently deliver, come rain or shine, without any added cost to the nostalgic taste of India.

Whether considering the *Mahabharata* analogy or Amul's strategy, one thing is clear. An unbreachable moat is a competitive advantage that separates the winners from the rest.

MARKET LENS

In the financial world, the concept of a moat was popularized by Warren Buffett, who likens a company to a castle surrounded by a wide, defensive moat that shields it from competitors. The wider and stronger the moat, the more difficult it is for competitors to storm the castle; and the safer your investment becomes.

Now, imagine if Arjun had opted for Shri Krishna's mighty army instead of Shri Krishna himself. On paper, the army appeared impressive — big, powerful and intimidating.

However, without Shri Krishna's strategy and foresight, the Arjun could have been outwitted at every turn. Even in the stock market, it's easy to be dazzled by a company's surface appeal, i.e., sales growth, market share, or flashy products. But without a moat, these factors can collapse faster than a poorly built sandcastle at high tide.

Let's discuss IRCTC (Indian Railway Catering and Tourism Corporation). It is a prime example of a company with an almost impenetrable moat. IRCTC has a monopoly-like position, managing ticketing, catering, and tourism for Indian Railways. This exclusive access has rendered the company nearly untouchable. Since going public in 2019, IRCTC's stocks have produced staggering returns, because when you control the tracks, competitors can't even board the train.

Did You Know ?

The word 'moat' comes from medieval castles, where a water-filled ditch protected against invaders. In investing, a moat serves the same purpose, shielding companies from competitors and market threats.

Another great example is CDSL (Central Depository Services Limited), which commands about 60% of the market share for depository services in India. As one of only two depositories in the country, CDSL is as essential to the financial market as a motherboard is to a computer. Its advantage lies not only in its leading position, but also in its indispensability. Any attempt to disrupt its position would be akin to trying to rewrite the fundamental rulebook governing the market operations.

Globally, the competitive advantages, or moats, shine even brighter. Companies like Coca-Cola and PepsiCo are well-known brands that dominate the beverage industry. Their strong distribution networks and high customer loyalty act as their moats, making it nearly impossible for new entrants to capture a significant share of the market. Imagine how hard it would be to convince a die-hard *chai* lover to switch to *kombucha*, a truly difficult endeavour.

Then there's ASML, a Dutch semiconductor equipment company. ASML is the only company in the world that manufactures extreme ultraviolet (EUV) lithography machines, which are a crucial component in advanced semiconductor production. Its moat? A proprietary technology that is yet to be imitated by any competitor. ASML is so far ahead of the game that it feels like it's playing a completely different game.

However, moats, can evolve, or erode over time. Moats are dynamic; what may provide a competitive advantage today could become a company's biggest weakness tomorrow. Take traditional retail banking as an example. A decade ago, banks like SBI, with more than 22,000 branches, enjoyed a considerable moat. But the rise of fintech companies has changed the game. With digital wallets, UPI, and app-based banking, physical branches have shifted from being a strength to becoming a liability. What was once a moat is now seen as a burden. It is crucial for investors to evaluate not just the existence of a moat, but also its sustainability in an ever-changing market.

To facilitate this process, let me introduce you to the **M.O.A.T.** framework. It's a straightforward yet effective way to assess a company's competitive advantage. Think of **M.O.A.T.** as an acronym that breaks down into four key elements:

M: MARKET POSITION

- Does the company dominate its market, or does it occupy a unique position?
- **Look Out For:** Monopoly-like control (e.g. IRCTC's rail services) or a significant market share (e.g. CDSL's role in depository services).

O: OPERATIONAL EFFICIENCY

- Is the company positioned to implement its strategy cost-effectively?
- **Look Out For:** Companies with streamlined operations and efficient processes, such as Amul's seamless supply chain or D-Mart's low-cost model.

A: ADAPTABILITY

- Can the company adapt to market changes and remain relevant?
- **Look Out For:** Strategic realignments such as Exide Industries' expansion into lithium-ion batteries.

T: TECHNOLOGICAL EDGE

- Does the company possess its own unique technology that sets it apart?
- **Look Out For:** Companies with cutting-edge technology, such as ASML's EUV lithography machines, that the competition can't replicate.

FROM MY JOURNEY

In my investment journey, finding companies with strong moats has been like discovering hidden gems during a treasure hunt, i.e., it's exciting, rewarding, and sometimes unexpected. For instance, I've invested in IRCTC, HAL (Hindustan Aeronautics Limited), and MCX (Multi Commodity Exchange), all of which have a firm position in their respective industries. But one investment that truly stood out was IRCTC. The experience left a lasting impression and reshaped how I view strategic investments.

On the day its IPO was announced, I happened to be travelling by train; talk about irony! As I held my IRCTC ticket in my hand, I thought, *"This company practically dominates train ticketing and catering"*. As I researched more about its near monopoly it became clear that new competitors would struggle to enter the market. The IPO was oversubscribed faster than a Diwali mega-sale, but I was determined not to miss out. By sheer luck, I was allotted a few stocks; my own *ticket* (pun intended) to what I hoped would be a profitable journey.

The stock was trading at ₹640 in October 2019. Within a few months, IRCTC surged past ₹1,200. I exited my position in February 2020 and the timely profit felt like discovering a hidden bonus in your salary slip. This experience prompted me to closely examine other companies with unassailable advantages. Here's an entry from *My Investment Diary:*

My Investment Diary

Today, I booked profits from my investment in IRCTC's stocks and earned over 100% in just a few months. I chose to invest in the company because I believed its monopoly in selling train tickets would keep competition at bay and the stock's performance validated the strength of this advantage.

This experience confirmed an important lesson in the power of a strong moat.

Debit: "Increased confidence in the strength of a broad economic moat"
Credit: "Gains from investment in IRCTC stocks"
(Net balance: A wiser investor with stronger conviction in the strength of moats when selecting stocks)

25 Feb 2020
(Tuesday)

THE BOTTOM LINE

A strong moat is not merely an attribute; it is the foundation that ensures a company's resilience and long-term success. Whether it's IRCTC's monopoly in rail transportation, CDSL's indispensability in financial markets, or Amul's steadfast cooperative model, moats create a layer of defence that contributes to long-term success.

No moat is everlasting; evolving technologies and changing markets can transform yesterday's strengths into today's weaknesses if a company fails to adapt.

As an investor, your task is not just to identify companies with moats, but also to assess their sustainability. Is the company innovating to stay ahead? Is its competitive advantage still relevant in today's market? These questions distinguish good investments from great ones.

Ultimately, investing in businesses with sustainable moats is akin to choosing Shri Krishna in the *Mahabharata*. It may not seem like the obvious choice initially, but it leads to long-term victory. A strong moat protects your portfolio from market turbulence and ensures that your investments grow steadily over time. Therefore, when assessing a stock, remember — the bigger the moat, the safer the castle.

A tree with strong roots laughs at storms.

- Malay Proverb

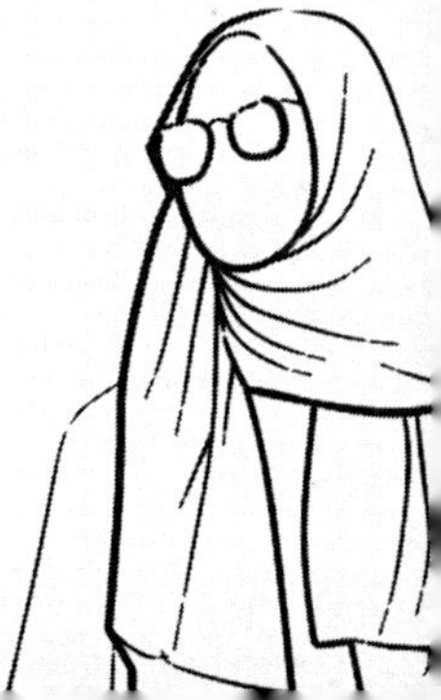

6

IN LEADERS WE TRUST

If you had to bet on a cricket match, would you go with a team of star players or a captain who can outthink the opposition?

Cricket is more than just a sport in India; it is practically another religion. In every corner of the country, from the bustling streets of Mumbai to the calm waters of Kerala, from the snow-capped peaks of Himachal to the lush tea gardens of Assam, children swing their bats with everything from tennis balls to coconuts. It's not just a game; it's a national obsession that brings a billion people together, even if we can't agree on who gets to bat first.

My love affair with cricket began in the early 2000s, during what can only be described as the soap opera phase of Indian cricket. The match-fixing scandal had shaken the team to its foundations, disillusioning fans and plunging the sport into crisis. Then came Sourav Ganguly, the Prince of Calcutta, who transformed chaos into a comeback story to rival any Bollywood blockbuster. He was a captain with the charisma of a leading actor, the strategy of a chess grandmaster, and the aggression of a gully cricket champion. Under his leadership, India evolved from a team of *"almost"* players to one that could even make Steve Waugh's unbeatable Australians sweat. Waugh once said, *"When Ganguly's in the lineup, you know it's game on".* That's the kind of leadership that not only wins games but also rewrites history.

The highlight of Ganguly's captaincy was the 2003–04 tour of Australia. Back then, Australia ruled world cricket and backing India felt like betting on a rickshaw in a Formula One race. But Ganguly had other plans. He backed young players like Yuvraj Singh and Virender Sehwag, who brought the swag to cricket long before it was even a thing. The result? India not only held Australia to a 1-1 draw, but also sent a message loud enough to echo across continents. Indian cricket wasn't here to join in; it was here to take over.

Ganguly's charisma only grew with time and who can forget his legendary shirt wave at Lord's? Oh, that glorious moment of defiance that screamed, *"We're not just here to play by the rules; we're here to break them!"* However, Ganguly's real magic wasn't just in his iconic gestures; it was in the way he transformed a group of talented individuals into a unified, relentless winning machine. He didn't merely lead a team; he inspired an entire generation. Under his leadership, India laid the foundation for its golden era, with leaders like MS Dhoni and Virat Kohli taking up the baton and carrying it forward; in Kohli's case, sometimes literally.

MARKET LENS

Just as Sourav Ganguly's leadership gave Indian cricket a new identity; visionary leadership can transform a company from an ordinary market player into an industry leader. A great leader is like a great captain in cricket; someone who knows how to overcome challenges, inspire the team, and turn seemingly impossible situations into opportunities.

Take, for example, the story of the Ambani brothers. In 2005, Reliance Industries was split between Mukesh and Anil Ambani, with each taking control of different businesses. Mukesh Ambani took over the oil, gas, and petrochemicals, while Anil Ambani was in charge of telecom, power, and entertainment. What followed was a master class in leadership. Mukesh Ambani didn't just run his companies; he revolutionized them. His bold decisions such as founding Reliance Jio, turned the telecom industry upside down, brought crores of people online, and made data cheaper than *chai*. Under his leadership, Reliance diversified into retail, digital services, and green energy, becoming a global powerhouse. The contrast is stark. One brother steered his ship to unimagined heights while the other struggled to stay afloat. The difference? Leadership qualities.

Let's also discuss another name synonymous with great leadership in the Indian business world: Radhakishan Damani, the founder of D-Mart and a prominent value investor. His approach to retail was simple, but ingenious as he focused on cost efficiency, kept the shopping experience no-frills and passed on the savings to the customers. Damani didn't just build a retail chain; he built a legacy. Under his disciplined leadership, D-Mart expanded rapidly to become one of India's largest and most profitable retail chains. For investors, it was a real jackpot. D-Mart's IPO in 2017 delivered outstanding returns and proved that backing the right leader pays off.

This phenomenon isn't limited to India. Around the world, leaders like Elon Musk, Jeff Bezos, and Satya Nadella have demonstrated shown how visionary leadership can transform companies into market giants. Musk's bold thinking has made Tesla, the market leader in electric vehicles. Bezos has redefined global e-commerce with Amazon and Nadella has revitalized Microsoft, leading it to supremacy in cloud computing.

Leadership is not just a "nice-to-have" for companies; it is the most crucial factor to consider. A great leader can transform crises into opportunities, inspire teams to excel, and guide the organization towards long-term success.

Understanding the importance of leadership is one thing, but applying this knowledge to assess its quality and make investment decisions is another. Here are some practical steps to help you identify companies with strong leadership:

- **Research the executive's track record:** Investigate the background of the CEO or founder. Have they successfully overcome challenges in the past? Are they recognized for getting results?
- **Listen to earnings announcements:** Earnings releases are a goldmine for understanding a leader's vision and strategy. Do they outline clear goals?
- **Pay attention to strategic decisions:** Examine recent moves, such as acquisitions, expansions, or new product launches. Great leaders make bold yet calculated decisions that position the company for future success.
- **Observe the employee culture:** Leadership isn't solely about what the CEO says, it's also about how they inspire their team. Check reviews on platforms like Glassdoor or LinkedIn to understand employee sentiment

- **Assess execution capabilities:** A great leader doesn't just make big promises; they deliver results. Monitor whether the company is achieving its goals and how well its strategies are being implemented.

Pro Tip

If the CEO sounds more like a motivational speaker than someone who has a plan, you should be careful.

Let's also talk about a different perspective. What happens when an important leader leaves? Imagine Jasprit Bumrah announcing shortly before the final of the 2024 World Cup, that he would no longer be playing. Chaos breaks out. The team, or, in this case, the company is on the verge of struggling, because it lacks confidence in its ability to succeed without its star player. Remember when Jeff Bezos stepped down as CEO of Amazon? Investors felt like a cricket team without a captain, questioning whether the new leadership could deliver the same kind of knock-out performance that Bezos had consistently provided. But when that leader leaves, it's essential to assess whether the new captain can navigate the ship effectively or if it is at risk of capsizing due to poor planning.

FROM MY JOURNEY

In my investing journey, I've always seen leadership as the defining ingredient, the element that can transform even a bland recipe into a Michelin-starred meal. My experience with Marksans Pharma has only reinforced this belief.

Let's go back to 2022. Marksans was not exactly a market favourite; it wasn't making headlines or generating buzz in the Telegram stock groups. Then, I came across the CEO, Mark Saldanha, during an earnings call. His presentation of the company's long-term strategy was captivating, much like a master chef explaining the meticulous art of making the perfect *biryani* — detailed, careful, and infused with a quiet confidence that assured me, *"Trust me, this will pay off"*.

Mr. Saldanha happens to be the brother of Glen Saldanha, the head of Glenmark Pharma. It felt like a classic sibling rivalry; reminiscent of the Ambani brothers, just in lab coats. It was clear that Mr. Mark not only wanted to lead his company but also to prove that his venture could compete with his brother's big-league enterprise. That spark of competition ignited my interest.

At the time, Marksans was trading at around ₹60, which felt like a bargain, like finding your favourite brand on sale at 50% off. So, I decided to invest not just based on the company's fundamentals but also in its leadership. It was like rooting for the underdog in a Bollywood movie; the character who may start slowly, but ultimately ends up outshining everyone when the climax hits.

Over the following years, Mark Saldanha not only met expectations but surpassed them. Through strategic acquisitions, global expansions, and consistent performance Marksans became a compelling story. By 2024, the stock had more than quadrupled and was trading at ₹270. It was reminiscent of a side character in a TV drama transforming into the surprising main character; unexpected but wholly satisfying.

Of course, not everything went smoothly. There were days when the market was more unpredictable than a three-year-old at bedtime. However, what reassured me was Mr. Saldanha's clear vision. Every time he talked about the company's direction, I felt like I was hearing a GPS voice saying, *"You're on the right track"*. No drama, no detours; just a steady march towards the goal.

When I finally booked profits at ₹250, it felt like receiving a *"Congratulations! Your order has been delivered"* notification after months of anticipation. The fundamentals were undoubtedly solid, but the real reason for the company's transformation was its leadership. Mr. Mark wasn't just running Marksans; he was building a legacy. Here's an entry from *My Investment Diary:*

My Investment Diary

Today, I booked profits in Marksans Pharma at around ₹250 after watching its stock price rise from ₹60 in 2021. Strong leadership and smart expansions have fuelled this growth and it feels like a well-deserved reward for trusting a CEO to execute his vision.

This experience has taught me the importance of good leadership. Selecting the right leader is crucial to choosing the right stock.

Debit: "The conviction that strong leadership can reshape the future of a company"
Credit: "Profits from the sale of Marksans pharma stocks"
(Net balance: A smart investor who understands the importance of leadership in a company)

12 Sep 2024
(Thursday)

THE BOTTOM LINE

When you invest in a company, you are not only buying its stocks but also its leadership. Think of it as choosing a flight. While the condition of the aeroplane (the fundamentals) is important, if the pilot (the leader) doesn't know how to handle turbulence, you're in for a rough flight.

Now, circling back to the cricket question I asked at the beginning: would you back a team full of stars or a team with an outstanding captain? The truth is that you need both. A team without stars is like a recipe missing key ingredients; it just won't work. But even with all the stars in the world, a team without an outstanding captain is like a headless chicken

— lots of potential but no direction. I don't mean to downplay the importance of the team, but a great leader is often the glue that holds everything together, the force that transforms raw talent into a winning machine. In both cricket and business, leadership is a crucial factor.

Great leaders not only manage companies; they change them. They see opportunities where others see obstacles, turn crises into comebacks, and inspire their teams to deliver results that make investors smile. Leaders like Mukesh Ambani, Radhakishan Damani and Mark Saldanha don't just build companies; they create a legacy.

This chapter's title, "In Leaders We Trust", borrows from the phrase "In God We Trust" printed on U.S. currency. If the dollar reflects faith in a nation, investing rests on faith in leadership. A great leader can turn an average company into a market giant. Without one, even the best business can crumble.

So, before you invest, ask yourself: Who is steering the ship? If the answer fills you with confidence, you are on the right track. After all, we trust leaders and with the right ones, your investments can go from ordinary to extraordinary.

Vision without action is a daydream.
Action without vision is a nightmare.

- Japanese Proverb

THE 3-PLATE PORTFOLIO

Have you ever convinced yourself that "this time it's different", only to realize later that it was the same old mistake waiting to happen?

Imagine a scenario: It's Friday evening. You and your friends are finally done with work and want to treat yourselves after a long week. As you enter a fancy restaurant, you're greeted by an irresistible buffet that could tempt even the strict dieters. Buttery *naan,* smoky *paneer tikka,* rich *dal makhani,* fragrant *biryani,* every dish looks more tempting than the next. Your stomach growls, your taste buds dance in anticipation, and for a moment, life feels perfect.

Now, imagine ignoring all these delicious options and stubbornly ordering just one dish: *Dal Makhani.* You've convinced yourself that this is the best choice, but what if today's dal is bland? Too watery? Too salty? Suddenly, your long-awaited dinner is ruined. With no substitute and no plan B, disappointment is all that's left on your plate.

On the other hand, if you had opted for the buffet, a bad dish wouldn't have been such a disaster. Maybe the *paneer tikka* steals your heart, or the biryani turns out to be the star of the evening. By spreading your choices across several dishes, you ensure that your evening remains a culinary success.

The stock market operates in the same way. Betting everything on a single stock is like ordering just one dish; you put all your faith (and money) into something that may or may not live up to expectations. However, if you wisely diversify your investments, one bad stock can't spoil the entire experience.

MARKET LENS

You've probably heard the saying, *"Don't put all your eggs in one basket"* countless times. Think about how many times Ranbir Kapoor says *"Papa"* in Animal, that's how many times I'm willing to repeat that phrase. Yet, let's be honest; many of us still love the idea of a "sure thing". We convince ourselves that we've found the next HDFC Bank, Reliance, and Bajaj Finance, and before we know it, we have most of our portfolio invested in one or two stocks.

But here's the reality. No company, no matter how strong it is, can guarantee returns forever. Even the best companies can be affected by sudden downturns due to regulatory changes, economic slowdowns, corporate scandals, or *Black Swan*[24] events *(hello, COVID-19!)*. If you invest all your money into a single stock, you leave yourself completely vulnerable.

Imagine putting every rupee you have into a single company, perhaps a booming IT giant. Everything looks great — sales are rising, profits are solid, and management seems to be making

[24] Black Swan is defined as an unforeseen, rare, and high-impact event (for example, the COVID-19 pandemic). In investing, a black swan can cause sudden market downturns. Because these events are unpredictable, they highlight the risk of over-concentrating investments.

all the right moves. Then, *BOOM!* A major global recession hits, tech stocks plummet, and suddenly your "guaranteed winner" has dropped by 60%. If you had instead spread your money across sectors like IT, banking, FMCG, and pharma, or even included gold and bonds, the crash would have been far less painful.

Diversification is your financial lifeline. If one investment fails, others can compensate for it. Just like a buffet needs a mix of flavours; some spicy, some mild, some sweet to enjoy the food. Similarly, your portfolio should contain a mix of stocks, bonds, and other investments to ensure smooth, long-term growth.

So, how do you build a balanced portfolio? Say hello to my 3-Plate Buffet Rule.

THE 3-PLATE BUFFET RULE

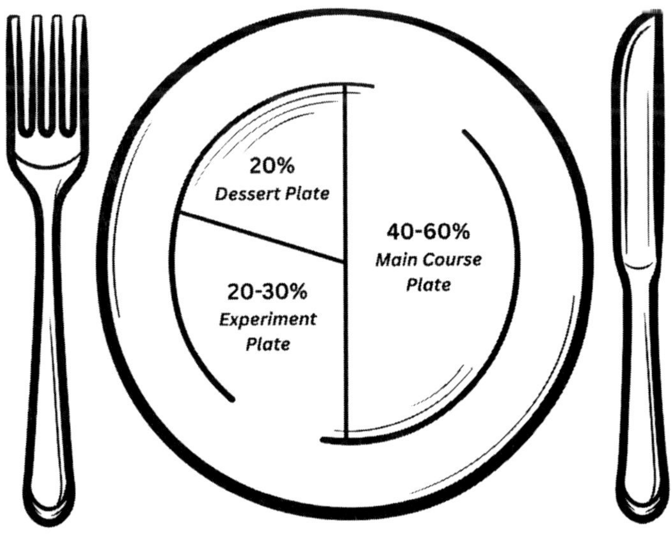

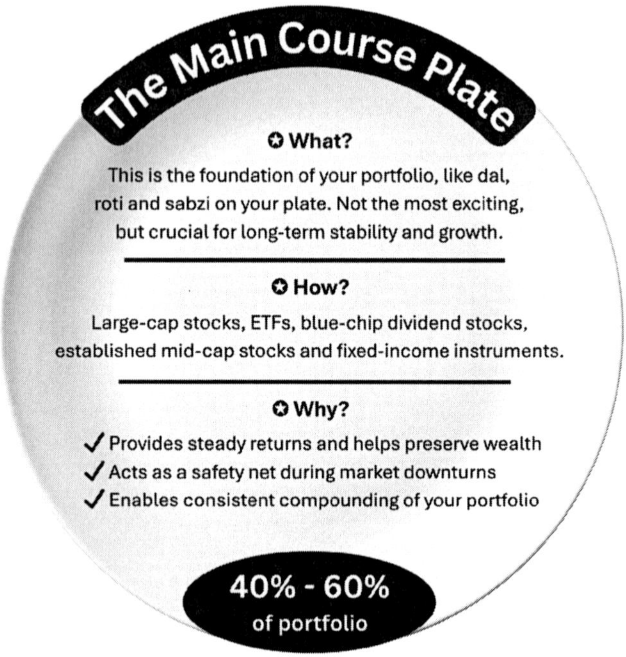

25

---

[25] Large-Cap: Shares of a large company with a high market capitalization. These companies are typically well-established, stable, and often leaders in their industries.

Index funds: A type of mutual fund or ETF designed to replicate the performance of a market index (like the Nifty 50 or S&P 500) by holding all (or a representative sample) of the index's constituent investments.

ETFs: An investment fund that trades on stock exchanges like a stock. It holds a basket of assets (stocks, bonds, etc.) and typically tracks an index, combining the diversification of a fund with the tradability of a stock.

Blue-Chip: Stock of a well-established, financially sound, and historically reliable company. Blue-chip companies (often large-caps) are known for quality and stability, and many pay regular dividends.

Mid-Cap: Shares of a medium-sized company with a moderate market capitalization. These firms have potential for growth but are generally less stable than large-caps and less risky than small-caps.

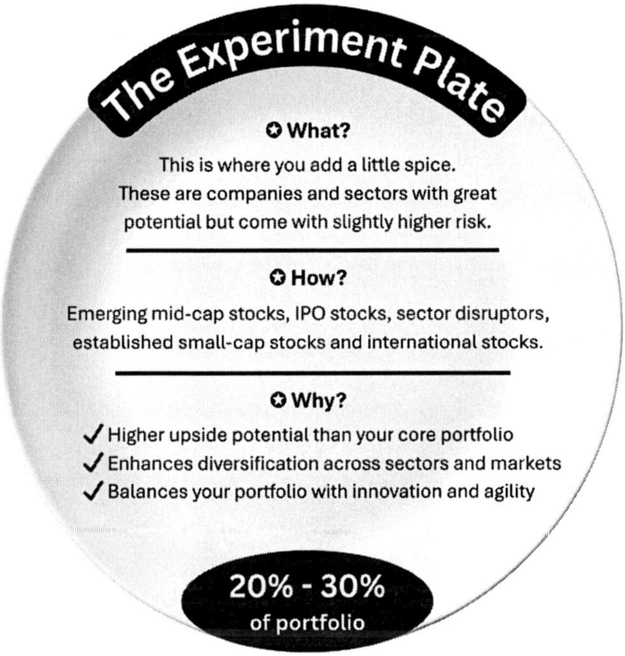

Bond: A fixed-income security representing a loan made by an investor to a borrower (typically corporate or government). A bond pays periodic interest and returns the principal at maturity generally less risky than stocks.

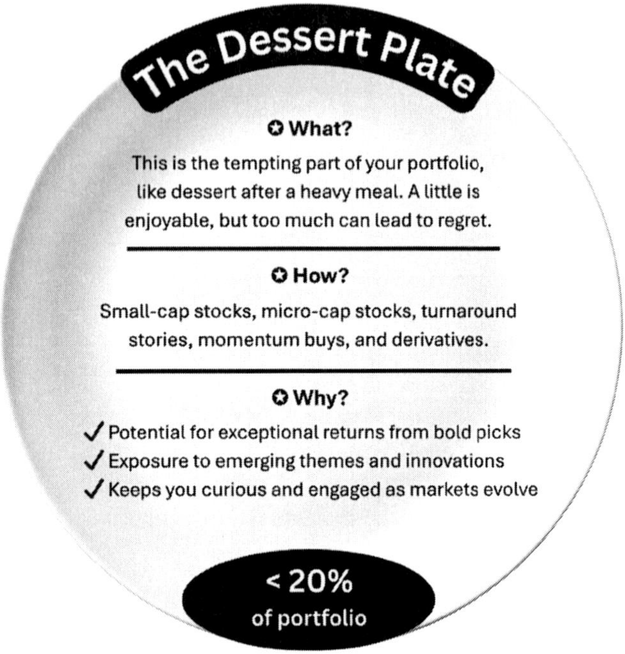

[26]

FROM MY JOURNEY

A few years ago, I discovered a stock called Andhra Papers — a *"hidden gem"* in the packaging industry. At that time, it was trading at a remarkably low P/E ratio of 4–5x, while most stocks in the market hovered around 30x or more. The paper industry was in a downturn, but I saw this as a once-in-a-lifetime opportunity, a fundamentally strong company at a bargain price!

---

[26] Small-Cap: Shares of a smaller company with a low market capitalization. These stocks can offer high growth potential but also come with higher volatility and risk.

Derivative: A financial instrument whose value is derived from an underlying asset or benchmark. Examples include futures, options, and swaps. Derivatives are used for hedging risk or for speculative investment.

I did my homework. I read financial reports and analysed industry trends. Everything indicated a strong BUY. However, here's where I made my mistake. I didn't just buy; I went all in.

Convinced I had struck gold, I allocated 80% of my portfolio to Andhra Papers. For a few weeks, the stock performed well and I felt like an investment genius. *"This is it! My big break!"* Yes, I had been warned about the importance of diversification countless times before, but my overconfidence insisted, *"This time it's different"*.

Then came the crash. A workers' strike halted production for months, the cost of raw materials skyrocketed and my "golden pick" plummeted overnight. My overconfidence had cost me dearly. Here's an entry from *My Investment Diary:*

My Investment Diary

Today, I had to watch my investment in Andhra Papers collapse due to a production strike. My big bet backfired, and I lost severely. I should have diversified instead of putting everything into a single stock.

This experience has taught me an important lesson. Never put all your eggs in one basket, no matter how promising it may seem.

Debit: "Substantial loss due to an over-concentrated bet on Andhra Papers"
Credit: "A hard-earned lesson on the importance of diversification in a portfolio"
(Net balance: A cautious investor who has understood the importance of diversification)

20 Dec 2019
(Friday)

Now, whenever I get overly excited about a stock, my mind screams, *"Andhra Papers! Andhra Papers!"* and I snap back to reality. Diversification is not just a theory; it's a survival *mantra.*

Quick Hack

Conduct an audit of your portfolio once a year to ensure that you do not exceed the allocation limits.

THE BOTTOM LINE

The stock market can be unpredictable and even the best stocks can face unexpected obstacles. A well-diversified portfolio ensures that you can stay afloat with other stocks when one investment takes a downturn. By following the "3-plate buffet rule", you can avoid being overly invested in a single stock and prevent regrets from an all-or-nothing bet.

So, the next time you're tempted to invest heavily in a stock, ask yourself, *"Would I do the same with a buffet?"* If the answer is no, make sure to diversify your investments wisely; your portfolio (and your future self) will thank you.

To put everything on one card and expect to win is to invite fortune to play dice with your fate.

- Friedrich Schiller
(German playwright and poet)

DECODING THE 8TH WONDER

What insignificant habit or decision did you make without much thought, only to realize later that it had a profound impact on life?

Let's play a quick game. What do a humble man of the woods, a mountaineering legend, and a seemingly boring math formula have in common? It sounds like the template for a bizarre joke, doesn't it? But trust me, the punchline will change the way you think about wealth forever.

First, meet Jadav Payeng. No, he's not a Bollywood hero, but his story is more inspiring than half the movies we see. In 1979, Payeng noticed that deforestation was turning a part of Assam into a wasteland. Instead of complaining about it (like most of us do about potholes or rising vegetable prices), he took a handful of saplings and started planting. All by himself!

They mocked him. Called him mad. But he didn't stop. What began as a one-man mission with a few saplings is now *Molai Forest,* a sprawling 1,360-acre jungle teeming with elephants, tigers, and thousands of other wild creatures. That's right. He single-handedly grew a forest.

Then there is Dashrath Manjhi, also known as the Mountain Man. After losing his wife because the nearest hospital was 55 km away, he picked up a hammer and chisel, and did something that would put even Sunny Deol in *Gadar* movie to shame; he started digging a road through a mountain. No fancy equipment, no government grants, just tireless labour. It took him 22 years, but when he was done, the road had shortened the distance between his village and the hospital to 15 km.

So, what is the secret sauce in these stories?

Small, consistent actions that lead to extraordinary results. And if you think this only applies to jungles and mountains, wait until you see what it does to your portfolio. Because my friend, this is the same principle that Albert Einstein referred to as the 8th wonder of the world: *Compounding!*

The only problem? Most of us underestimate it, ignore it, or even worse, get bored before it works. But once you understand its power, you'll never view money the same way again. Are you ready to uncover the true secret of the 8th wonder? Then, let's dive in.

MARKET LENS

Payeng's saplings and Manjhi's hammer teach us that success is not born overnight but is built step by step. The same principle applies to investing. Small, consistent actions can turn into life-changing wealth through the power of compounding. It's not about dramatic overnight success but about consistent efforts, patience, and a willingness to stick to the plan.

If those words sound too nerdy, don't worry, I promise this isn't a math lecture. But answer me this, *"If you start with just ₹1 and double that amount every day for 30 days, how much do you think you'll have at the end of the month?"*

Most people estimate a few thousand. Some even assume one or two lakhs. But, on the 30th day, this ₹ 1 turns into an incredible ₹ 53.68 crore. Yes, let that sink in. This is not magic. It's just the effect of compounding — small, steady investments that turn into something significant over time.

But most people never experience this magic. The reason? They don't stay invested long enough. They get impatient, want quick results, and if they don't see profits immediately, they give up. Investing isn't a lottery where you strike gold overnight; it's a slow-cooked biryani that takes time to absorb the flavours. It may feel like you're watching paint dry, i.e., your investment doesn't seem to be yielding much. But if you wait long enough, you'll reach a point where the *compounding* effect kicks in and that's when the real magic happens.

Let's put this to the test. I want you to meet two friends — Ramesh and Suresh. No, not the guys from the *Cadbury 5 Star* commercial, but equally clueless when it comes to investing.

At the age of 25, Ramesh begins investing ₹10,000 a month. He sticks to this plan and remains undeterred by market fluctuations, simply continuing to invest. Suresh, on the other hand, has a different strategy. With a YOLO mindset and a *Zindagi Na Milegi Dobara* playlist, he keeps telling himself, *"I'll invest when I'm rich".*

Fast forward 10 years. Suresh finally realizes that he should have started earlier. To make up for lost time, he now invests twice as much, i.e., ₹ 20,000 per month, but he only begins this from the age of 35. Now, I'll pose the question to you, *"Who do you think will have more wealth at the age of 55?"*

Most people instinctively say Suresh. After all, he is investing double the amount, so his wealth should be higher, right?

Wrong. Although Suresh has invested twice as much, he ends up with less money than Ramesh. Why? Because Ramesh's investments have had 10 years more to compound. In the stock market, time beats money.

This is where most investors go wrong. They focus too much on how much they invest and too little on how long they invest. The truth is that compounding doesn't care itself about how rich you are; it only matters how early you start. For every year you delay, you lose a compounding cycle. The earlier you start, the more often your money doubles and the bigger your wealth snowball becomes.

So how can you make compounding work for you? It's quite simple. Follow the **T.I.M.E.** principle:

T - Time in the market: Start early and stay invested as long as possible. The biggest advantage lies not in picking the best stocks, but in allowing time to work for you.

I - Invest consistently: Wealth is not created in one fell swoop. Set up a regular schedule, make investing a habit, and do it month after month, year after year, whether the market is high or low.

M - Minimize withdrawals: The greatest enemy of compounding is withdrawing your money too early. Allow your investments to grow undisturbed. Don't treat your portfolio like an ATM. Plan your withdrawals wisely.

E - Extend the time horizon: Think in terms of decades, not years. The stock market rewards those who take a long-term view. The longer you hold your investments, the higher your return.

Compounding is a test of patience, not intelligence. It's about having the discipline to stay invested and let time do the heavy lifting. The real difference between those who build lasting wealth and those who don't lies not in knowledge alone, but also in patience.

The only question that remains is, *"Are you patient enough to make compounding work for you, or will you be like Suresh, forever waiting for the 'right time' that never comes?"*

FROM MY JOURNEY

Let me take you back to April 2017. A simpler time when our biggest worries were taking *chai* breaks at the office and figuring out how to make the most of free food at company events. My friend Ankit and I, newly qualified Chartered Accountants (CA), had just started our first jobs with modest salaries and big dreams. One day, over another cup of *chai,* Ankit sighed, *"Why is my savings account growing fatter while my investment account looks like it's on a diet?"*

That got us thinking. We had both learned about investing in theory, but our current portfolios looked like deserted islands, i.e., untouched and forgotten. After brainstorming over *chai* (because all good financial decisions are made over *chai,* right?), we came up with a simple plan to consistently invest in solid stocks month after month, regardless of market conditions. No market timing or sophisticated stock picking but just pure consistency.

We jokingly called it the "SIP[27] of shares" because we committed to buying a few stocks each month. The rules were simple:

☑ Every payday, we bought five stocks each of L&T, Bajaj Finance, and Tata Elxsi.

☑ No overthinking and no panic selling; just buy and hold.

While our friends bragged about the latest gadgets, weekend getaways, and overpriced coffee, we adhered to our routine as if it were a sacred ritual. Payday wasn't just about salary credits; it was about logging in, placing our stock orders, and then celebrating with a cutting *chai.*

Of course, like any good Bollywood drama, our journey was not without its twists and turns. The market had its ups and downs, sharp crashes, euphoric rallies, and days that felt like a suspenseful thriller with no climax. Then came March 2020. COVID-19 hit and our portfolio crashed faster than the quality of comedy in recent Bollywood films (seriously, where are the good ones?).

---

[27] SIP is an approach to investing (especially common with mutual funds) where one invests a fixed amount at regular intervals, instead of in one lump sum. SIPs instil discipline and average out the purchase cost over time, reducing the impact of market volatility.

In that moment, self-doubt crept in. *"Have we messed up? Should we sell our stocks and cut our losses?"* The temptation was strong but the fundamentals were stronger. We recalled the golden rule of compounding — stay invested. So, we carried on.

And you know what? The market rebounded dramatically in a V-shaped recovery and our investments soared. The same stocks that had seemed like sinking ships in March 2020, surged like rockets by the end of the year.

Our little experiment has turned into something extraordinary. What started as a small investment over a *chai* has grown into a solid money now.

We still laugh about our "Chai Money", but the numbers are no joke; they have grown into something significant, illustrating the importance of sticking to a plan. To put things in perspective, let's look at how our investments have evolved over the years:

Evolution of "Chai Money" over the period

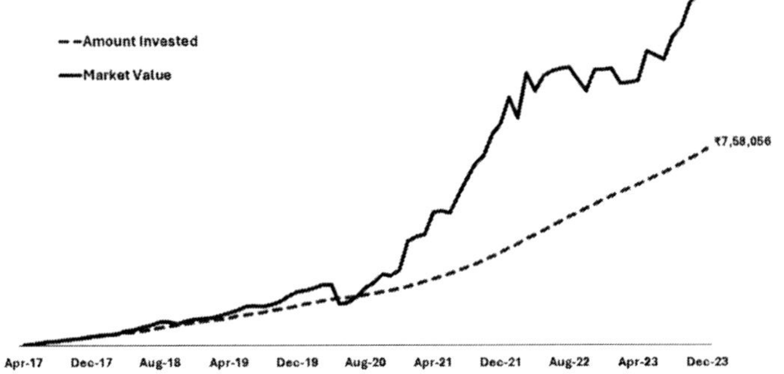

Reflecting on the year's journey, I wrote a letter to myself in *My Investment Diary* on December 31, 2023. It was a reminder that patience pays off and that compounding rewards those who trust the process.

My Investment Diary

Today, I looked back at our "SIP of Shares" experiment and was amazed at how much it has grown. Even during the stock market crash in 2020, we stuck to the plan, and now those same stocks are worth far more than we ever imagined.

The lesson is clear: patience and perseverance are not just strategies; they are the true drivers of long-term wealth.

Debit: "A lesson on the power of compounding and the effects of consistent investment"
Credit: "Steady gains from staying disciplined and sticking to the plan"
(Net balance: A strong belief in the magic of compounding and the patience it requires)

31 Dec 2023
(Sunday)

The lesson here is that the true winners in the stock market are not those who chase quick riches or react to every market movement. Rather, they are the investors who invest consistently, allow compounding to work its magic and understand that patience is the key. However, patience doesn't mean ignoring fair value.

When a stock has reached its fair price, it's perfectly acceptable to book profits and reinvest elsewhere. Think of it like tending to a garden — plant seeds (invest), water them (continually add funds), and sometimes prune back (exit) when necessary. Over time, these small, consistent actions can lead to remarkable results.

Quick Hack

Make investing your first expense each payday or day of earning. Choose a fixed percentage (e.g., 20%) of your income and invest it as soon as you receive your payment.

THE BOTTOM LINE

Lionel Messi once said, *"It took me 17 years and 114 days to become an overnight success".*

The stock market is no different. What appears to be an overnight success is often the result of years of discipline, patience, and unwavering commitment.

Investing is not about chasing quick profits, reacting to market noise, or making impulsive decisions based on WhatsApp stock tips. It's about planting the right seeds, nurturing them, and allowing time to work its magic.

Compounding, often referred to as the 8th wonder of the world, is not a mythical formula reserved for the super-rich or financial experts; it works for everyone if you dedicate time to it. The biggest challenge? Most people stop before compounding truly takes off. They lose patience, get distracted, or attempt to "get rich quick", only to find themselves back at square one. Compounding rewards those who stay committed to the journey.

Compounding is the eighth wonder of the world. He who understands it, earns it; he who doesn't, pays it.

- Albert Einstein
(German theoretical physicist)

THE DIVIDEND DELIGHT

Have you ever dreamed of earning something without working, just like receiving royalties from a hit song or renting out a property?

We all know the timeless fable of *"The Goose that Laid the Golden Eggs"*, which in Hindi is called *"Sone Ka Anda Dene Wali Murgi"*. The story is as old as time, but its lesson remains highly relevant. A simple farmer comes across a magical hen that lays a golden egg every day. *Jackpot!* A day's wages in gold without lifting a finger. Soon his wealth grows. He buys land, cattle, a bigger house, and soon becomes the richest man in the village. Life is good, perhaps too good.

But the more riches he accumulates, the more impatient he becomes. The thought of waiting for a single golden egg every day begins to irritate him. *"Why should I settle for one egg a day when I can have all the gold at once?"* Driven by greed, he makes the unthinkable decision to cut open the hen. But to his horror, he finds no treasure inside, just the normal intestines of a bird. The hen was like a machine that produced wealth. Instead of being patient, the farmer, consumed by FOMO, wanted everything at once. Following the motto *"shortcuts don't work"*, he ended up with nothing but chicken curry. In his desperation to get rich quickly, he destroyed the very thing that made him wealthy in the first place.

The usual moral of this story is that greed backfires. However, there's another, less appreciated lesson about investing. Sometimes, a steady stream of returns (the golden eggs) can be more valuable than the pursuit of instant wealth (the hen). This principle holds especially true in the world of dividends.

MARKET LENS

Dividend is the golden egg of investing. A dividend is simply a portion of a company's profits paid out to shareholders. They provide a steady stream of income while your investment (the stock itself) continues to grow. This arrangement allows you to profit from your stocks without having to sell them. It's like owning a mango tree that not only grows in value but also produces mangoes every season; why cut the tree down when you can enjoy the fruit year after year?

In the Indian stock market, several established companies with high dividend payouts have mastered the art of rewarding their shareholders. Companies like Indian Oil Corporation (IOC), Bharat Petroleum Corporation (BPCL), Coal India, ONGC, VST Industries, and Godfrey Phillips regularly share their profits.

Dividends are like the generous uncles of the stock market; they consistently provide cash, no questions asked. For instance, VST Industries has been delivering a dividend yield of around 5% annually in recent years. That's a solid yield, even if the stock price doesn't move an inch. Imagine earning this much just for holding a stock; it's like receiving a salary without having a boss. Plus, this yield often beats fixed deposit returns and unlike an FD, the stock also has the potential to grow in value, making it a win-win.

Dividends shine brightest during unpredictable market conditions. When stock prices are swinging wildly, like a tense cricket match in the last over, dividends act as your reliable batsman, ensuring you still receive returns even when the stock market throws a *googly.*

So, the next time someone brags about their multi-bagger stock, which may or may not take off, ask them, *"Brother, does your stock earn you anything while you hold it? No? Then let me enjoy my dividend checks while you wait for your jackpot".*

Did You Know ?

Some of the largest consumer brands in the world, such as Coca-Cola, P&G, and Nestlé; have consistently paid dividends for over 100 years without missing a single payment.

FROM MY JOURNEY

I have experienced the power of dividend investing firsthand. A part of my portfolio is invested in VST Industries, an established tobacco company. I know, I know… tobacco isn't exactly salad-for-the-soul stuff. But hey, while people burn cigarettes, I'll let my dividends smoke the charts. Year after year, I've received a steady *dividend yield*[28] of around 6-7%,

[28] Dividend Yield is annual dividend paid by a company divided by its current share price, expressed as a percentage. It shows how much cash return (dividend) an investor gets for each

providing me with a reliable income level from dividends alone.

The best part? In addition to this steady income, the stock has also increased in value over time. Imagine getting a *FD*[29] like return, but instead of locking your money away like your old-school uncle who doesn't trust the stock market, you benefit from the stock's appreciation as well. That's what dividend investing feels like — a combination of the best of both worlds. Below is a selection of established companies known for their strong dividend yields:

High Dividend Yield stocks

Dividend-paying companies may not enjoy the eye-catching stock price growth of tech companies or startups, but they offer something often underestimated, the predictability and stability.

---

rupee invested in the stock (e.g., a 5% yield means ₹5 per year for every ₹100 invested).

[29] Fixed Deposit, a savings/investment product offered by banks where money is deposited for a fixed term at a guaranteed interest rate. FDs (often a benchmark for "safe" returns) provide steady, low-risk interest income, but the money is locked in until maturity.

Many of these companies operate in sectors with reliable cash flows, such as oil and gas, tobacco, and utilities. While they may not be the next Tesla or Google, they consistently generate profits and share them with investors. Think of them as the responsible "elder siblings" in your portfolio; while riskier stocks are having wild adventures, these dividend stocks are quietly paying money into your account.

I've been a consistent investor in dividend stocks and have seen solid returns. Here's a snapshot from *My Investment Diary:*

My Investment Diary

Today, I received another dividend from VST Industries. It's not flashy, but it's consistent, and that consistency is important. I used to believe that only big price swings could lead to gains, but the dividends continue to add to my returns without me having to sell a single stock.

This is a great reminder that slow, steady compounding can be just as effective as market movements.

Debit: "Strong belief in the long-term value of dividend investing"
Credit: "Consistent passive income through steady dividend payouts"
(Net balance: An informed investor with greater conviction in the steady and reliable power of dividend)

13 Jul 2023
(Thursday)

Some people have taken dividend investing to a new level by carefully building portfolios of high-dividend stocks, earning tens of lakhs every year just from the dividends. Imagine never having to check the level of the Sensex again because your portfolio is providing you with a salary even when you're on vacation.

A common myth is that dividend investing is only for retired folks, but this couldn't be further from the truth. As a young investor, you don't have to cash out your dividends; you can reinvest them to buy more stocks, leading to a compounding effect over time. Reinvesting dividends is like using cheat codes for wealth. Your money starts making money, which in turn makes you more money. Before you know it, you're in a compounding loop, earning more passive income than your last salary hike. This is the snowball effect of dividend compounding, i.e., you earn dividends on your dividends, creating a passive income machine that grows larger every year.

In short, dividend investing enables your investments to work for you. With the right stocks, you can enjoy the benefits of both capital growth and dividend income, which can outperform many other investment strategies over the long term. After all, who wouldn't want an investment that literally pays them to hold it?

THE BOTTOM LINE

Dividends can be a powerful tool in your investment strategy when used wisely. For retired investors, a dividend-focused portfolio can provide a steady, reliable source of income to cover daily expenses. Think of it as a financial safety net, i.e., your stocks can increase in value while paying you regular dividends, all without having to sell a single stock. It's like owning rental properties that generate income without the need for sale.

For younger investors, dividends can be reinvested over time to purchase more stocks. By reinvesting dividends, you use the market's money to buy more stocks, leading to greater long-term gains. This is a simple yet effective way to grow your wealth.

All investors should consider including some dividend stocks in their portfolios, regardless of age or investment strategy. While the proportion may vary, including dividend stocks provides some cushion. As I always say, *"Profit wahi jo haath mein aaye"* (only profit that counts is the one you take home).

The moral of the story is clear. Don't harm the hen that lays golden eggs. Instead, nurture it, feed it well, and enjoy the golden eggs year after year. By maintaining the right balance between stock appreciation and dividend yield, you can build a robust, self-sustaining portfolio that serves you well in the long run, whether you seek regular income or long-term wealth accumulation.

So, the next time the stock market throws tantrums, don't panic just sip your *chai* and watch your dividends roll in.

The best time to plant a tree was 20 years ago. The second-best time is now.

- Chinese Proverb

10

HOLD RIGHT, SIT TIGHT

What is more difficult, making the right decision or sticking to it when the going gets tough?

I come from a farming family in Punjab, or as I like to say, agriculture is deeply rooted in me (pun intended!). From sunlit fields to the scent of freshly tilled soil, my connection to the land has always run deep. Growing up, I spent many of my childhood days at my Tau Ji's (my father's elder brother) house in the village. My brother and I spent hours in the fields and with my endless childhood curiosity, every visit came with a flood of questions.

Every time I saw the fields being sown; I'd bombard my Tau Ji with questions: *"What are we planting? How will it grow? When will we harvest?"*

I remember one such day during wheat sowing in November. As we walked through the fields, I eagerly asked, *"Tau Ji, when will we harvest the wheat? Tomorrow?"*

He laughed heartily and replied, *"No, it's not instant noodles, puttar!"* Then, with the patience of an experienced farmer, he explained (in Punjabi, of course, which I'm translating for you — because let's be real; I am not publishing this book exclusively for my cousins in Amritsar), *"Farming is about time and patience. You can't rush it. We've just sown the seeds. Now we wait, water the fields, give them sunlight, and let time do its work. Only after months of care will we reap the harvest".*

Naturally, my overactive brain switched into panic mode. *"But what if it rains too much? What if there's too much sun? What if the entire crop fails?"*

Tau Ji smiled knowingly and imparted a life lesson that I will never forget, *"Changa Leh, Tik ke Beh"*, which translates to *"Hold right and sit tight"*. We have done our part; now we must wait and trust the process.

This wisdom has stuck with me. Good things take time and it is unhelpful to rush into them. Whether in farming, investing, or even life itself, you need to put in the effort and have the patience to see results. In a world addicted to instant rewards, this lesson is more important than ever.

MARKET LENS

The peasant wisdom of Tau Ji — *"Hold right and sit tight"*; may have referred to crop, but it applies just as well to investing. In the stock market, as in agriculture, patience is rewarded and impatience is punished. The seeds of wealth are sown when you invest, but you need time, discipline, and perseverance to reap the rewards.

However, most investors behave like I did as a child in the wheat fields — restless, impatient, and constantly in search of the harvest. They want instant results, overnight returns, and shortcuts to riches. Great investments take time to compound, just as plants require time to grow.

If we talk in cricketing language, investing is a Test match, not a T20. You need the patience of Rahul Dravid at the crease, carefully defending and waiting for the right opportunity. You don't recklessly hit every ball for sixes. Instead, you pace your innings, play the long game, and let the market reward your perseverance over time.

Take Warren Buffett, for example. He didn't build his fortune by quickly switching stocks, but by holding good stocks for decades. In fact, almost 95% of his wealth was created after he turned 60. If that's not a testament to patience, I don't know what is!

Even in India, legendary investors like Rakesh Jhunjhunwala have held stocks like Titan for over two decades, witnessing their investments grow by 100 times or more. Imagine buying a stock and holding it until ₹ 1 lakh becomes ₹ 1 crore, yet most investors don't experience that because they panic at every small dip and exit too early.

Infosys is a classic example. Investors who have held the stock since its IPO in 1993 (when it was priced at just ₹ 95) have seen its value increase by over 1,50,000% in three decades! But how many people actually held on? Very few; most sold after doubling or tripling their money, missing out on the true power of compounding.

When the market becomes volatile, sometimes inaction is the best course of action. As the saying goes, *"Doing nothing is the hardest thing to do but often the smartest"*. Great investors wait for their stocks to mature and grow, much like a skilled hitter waits for the ball to enter their zone before hitting the big shots. The stock market is designed to transfer money from the impatient to the patient. Those who understand this simple principle build real wealth, while those who chase quick profits often end up regretting it.

Did You Know ?

Amazon's stock price dropped by more than 90% during the dot-com crash (1999-2001), yet those who persevered saw it become one of the most valuable companies in history.

FROM MY JOURNEY

When I started investing, I was the exact opposite of *"Hold right and Sit tight"*. I had the patience of a child waiting for a pizza delivery. I was constantly checking stock prices and desperate to trade. I thought that being active would lead to better returns, but I quickly learned that the real winners in the market are those who wait the longest, not those who trade the most.

One of the biggest tests of my patience on my investment journey was with ITC. For years, it was labelled a "dead stock", frustrating investors who expected quick profits. ITC remained in the ₹200-₹300 range for nearly seven years. If there was an award for the most trolled stock in the Indian market, ITC would have won it hands down.

I bought ITC stock for the first time in 2017 for around ₹200, using savings from my first salary. While it was a small amount, I always considered it "money well spent". My patience was tested for years as the stock barely moved and sat out every market rally. Many investors lost hope and jumped ship, but I held on. I believed in the company's strong fundamentals and was confident that, sooner or later, the market would recognise its true value.

Then came 2022. After years of no progress, ITC finally woke up and began to gain momentum. The same people who had once dismissed the stock as a laggard rushed to buy it. However, the biggest gains were not made by those who chased the rally, but by those who held on and remained patient. Here's an excerpt from *My Investment Diary:*

> *My Investment Diary*
>
> Today, I realized that ITC's stock has more than doubled after seven years of holding onto it. I had heard endless jokes about it never moving, but now those jokes have disappeared.
>
> This highlights a simple truth: The real market gains come to those who have the patience to wait.
>
> Debit: "A lesson in patience and staying invested despite market scepticism"
> Credit: "Worthwhile profits through the patient holding of ITC stocks"
> (Net balance: A disciplined investor with a stronger conviction to remain stable with solid fundamentals)
>
> **12 Jul 2023**
> **(Wednesday)**

A similar story has unfolded with Exide Industries and Amara Raja Batteries. For a long time, these stocks seemed stagnant and frustratingly slow, which led investors to doubt their potential. But once they began to rise, they became multi-baggers.

Patience pays off. Not every stock is a fast sprint; some are marathons. If the fundamentals are strong, sometimes you just have to trust the process and wait. The market doesn't reward impatience; it rewards conviction.

THE BOTTOM LINE

The stock market rewards those who wait. Patience is not just a virtue in life. It's the golden rule of investing. The biggest mistake investors make is getting out too early and expecting quick results from something that takes time to grow.

Just as pickles need time to develop their full flavour, your investments also need time to mature and compound. Like the wisdom of my Tau Ji in the fields, after sowing, it's often best to "Hold Right and Sit Tight". You don't dig up a plant every week to check if it's growing; you trust the process and let time work its magic.

The key is to focus on the long-term horizon. Short-term market fluctuations can tempt you to panic and get out, but history has shown that the best investors are those who keep a cool head and ride out their investments. Panic selling during a downturn is like leaving the cricket field in the middle of the game. Instead, play with the discipline of Rahul Dravid by being calm, patient, and always with an eye on the long game.

So, the next time the market fluctuates wildly, or your stock goes sideways for months, take a deep breath and remember you don't reap the crop before it's ripe; so why should you do the same with your investments?

The strongest of all warriors are these two: Time and Patience.

- Leo Tolstoy
(Russian novelist)

11

AAPDA ME AVSAR

Have you ever regretted not buying something when it was cheaper? What if you get that chance again — will you act or hesitate?

There are two kinds of shoppers in the world. Those who see a price tag and decide immediately and those who believe that no price is final until they've asked for a discount at least three times. I proudly belong to the second category.

When my wife and I were shopping for a blazer at H&M, our brains were already trained to spot discounts, just like a radar detects enemy planes. After some searching, we finally found the perfect blazer — stylish, comfortable, and just what she wanted. However, when we looked at the price tag, it read ₹12,000.

₹12,000 on a price tag? That's usually enough to activate our built-in discount radar. When it comes to discounts, religion, caste, and creed are irrelevant, only the percentage matters! Whether it's *Diwali Dhamaka, Eid Bonanza, Christmas Carnival, Guru Purab Mega Sale,* or even a *Tuesday Special Offer* that nobody understands, we are united in our hunt for a better deal. If there's one thing that truly unites India, it's not cricket, Bollywood, or even *biryani.* It's the shared instinct to never buy anything without first looking for a discount!

Naturally, we turned to the salesperson and asked the golden question, "*Kuch discount milega?*"

Unfortunately, we had no luck. The blazer was fresh in stock and there were no sales, no discounts, and no secret coupons. Just the harsh reality of retailing at full price. At this point, the only logical thing to do would have been to politely thank the salesperson and move on. But as anyone who has shopped with their spouse knows that, logic is an optional accessory in moments like this.

So, we decided to buy it anyway because I liked it very much. Just kidding, you don't argue about a 10% discount when peace at home is at stake.

But when I was making the payment, something magical happened at the cash counter. As the cashier scanned the item, the price suddenly dropped by 50%! My first thought? Wait, did I just gain secret VIP status for shoppers?

As it turned out, the store had just launched an unannounced flash sale and the blazer, which originally costed ₹12,000, was now mine for just ₹6,000!

For a moment, I stood there as if I had just discovered a hidden cheat code in real life. It was the kind of unexpected joy that feels like finding a ₹500 note in an old pair of jeans, i.e., pure, unexpected, and utterly delightful.

I realised that this thrill of getting something valuable at a bargain price is universal. Whether it's shopping, real estate, or the stock market, nothing compares to the joy of acquiring quality at a discount.

MARKET LENS

You know that thrill when you come across an unexpected discount? That feeling when what you want is suddenly 50% cheaper for no apparent reason? Well, here's the funny part, it happens in the stock market too.

Imagine a scenario! You have been tracking a stock for weeks. It has strong sales growth, excellent profit margins, solid management, and a promising future. But there's just one problem; the valuation is too high.

Would you rather pay the full price now or wait until it's on sale? Savvy investors know the answer and wait for the market version of an End of Season Sale (EOSS). And guess what? These stock market sell-offs happen more often than you might think.

When the market crashes, even the best stocks take an uninvited nosedive. It's as if H&M suddenly announces a 50% sell-off, making all the premium brands you couldn't afford finally within reach. The key difference? Most investors panic and run away from these discounts instead of taking advantage of them.

If you were anywhere near the stock market in March 2020, you know exactly what I mean. COVID-19 hit the world like an unexpected twist in a Bollywood movie. Sensex and Nifty collapsed faster than my willpower at a dessert buffet. In just a few weeks, stocks of fundamentally strong companies fell by 30-50%, not due to weak fundamentals, but due to sheer market panic.

March 23, 2020, was historic. The Sensex plunged 13% in a single day, triggering a *circuit breaker*[30] and halting trading. Even blue-chip stocks like HDFC Bank, TCS, and Reliance Industries traded at one-time discounts. Investors sold stocks like mango sellers rushing to offload ripe mangoes before they rot.

For experienced investors, this was not a crisis; it was a gold mine. And if there is one principle that applies to investing, it is this, "Aapda Me Avsar", the opportunity in disaster. When the dust settled, something fascinating happened:

- The stocks that had been tossed aside began to recover magnificently in the following months.
- Investors who bought during the panic saw their portfolios double (2x) or even triple (3x) within a year.
- Meanwhile, those who had sold out of fear were left watching the rally from the sidelines, regretting every moment.

The irony is that people flock to stores like Zara or Apple when there's a 50% off sale, as if it's their birthright. Yet, when the stock market collapses and stocks are available at a one-time discount, people run away in fear.

Why is that? Because human psychology is wired to avoid uncertainty.

- When the market rises, everyone wants to buy.
- When the market falls, panic sets in and people start selling.

---

[30] Circuit Breaker is a mechanism in stock exchanges to temporarily halt trading if a market index moves beyond a preset threshold in a short time (for example, a 10% one-day drop triggers a trading pause to curb panic selling).

What is the right approach? Buy when everyone else is scared. There will always be chaotic phases in the market, but if you train yourself to see opportunities in disaster, Aapda Me Avsar, then you will always be one step ahead of the game. Because investing is like shopping; you often find the best deals when no one else is looking for them.

FROM MY JOURNEY

March 2020 was a month that made even the most experienced investors question everything. While the world was busy hoarding hand sanitizer, Maggi, and other such useless things (why did everyone in India suddenly buy so much toilet paper?), the stock market experienced a historic slump.

The chaos wasn't limited to the markets. Do you remember the Janta curfew? That surreal Sunday when people stepped out onto their balconies and banged utensils together as if attempting to scare away a spirit rather than a virus? And who can forget the iconic video of a young lady dancing Bollywood-style and chanting *"Go Corona Go!"* as if COVID-19 would simply take offence and leave? Those were wild times.

But for investors like me, the real nightmare unfolded in our portfolios. I had been investing seriously for a few years and felt pretty good about it. My portfolio was in the green and I was even giving unsolicited stock tips to friends, which, in hindsight, should have been my first warning sign.

(Mistake # 1: Overconfidence).

Then came March 2020 and within just a few days my portfolio plummeted by 40-50%. Stocks I was confident about collapsed like a house of cards in a storm. The Sensex hit two lower circuits and for the first time in my investing journey, I felt real panic. Everywhere I turned, doom and pessimism prevailed. Groups, financial news channels, and YouTube 'experts' were all shouting the same thing:

"Nifty is going to 5,000!"

"Sell everything before it's too late!"

"Bro, buy gold! Or maybe real estate! Or should we just hoard atta-dal?"

At first, I tried to remain rational. But when you see your hard-earned money disappear at the speed of an IPL powerplay, rationality takes a back seat. I sold a large chunk of my stocks in June 2020 as I was convinced that the market would fall even further.

(Mistake # 2: Listening to panic-mongers).

One thing I realized from this is that history always looks logical in hindsight. But when you're living through it, it feels like absolute chaos, like trying to order from Subway for the first time.

Wait, before we go any further, I need to get this Subway rant off my chest first. Why do I have to name every vegetable? Just give me everything! And *jalapeño* — oh, so the "J" is silent? Great, just like our former Prime Minister!

One day, as I followed the stock market news, I noticed something interesting. The very people who had previously been shouting *"Sell everything!"* were now quietly buying stocks. The smart money experienced investors, fund managers, and seasoned traders, all were using this panic as an opportunity.

At that moment, I realised that this was not the end; it was a beginning. I had already made the mistake of selling and didn't want to make another mistake by holding back. I began buying quality stocks again, though this time out of conviction, not fear. Below is a snapshot of Nifty's movement during COVID, capturing the panic, fear, and a market in freefall:

Performance of Nifty during Covid-19 period

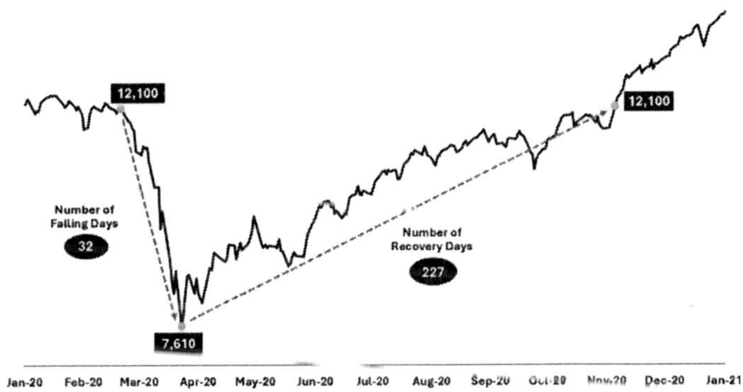

The stocks I bought after the chaos of 2021 turned out to be some of the best investments I've ever made. The market recovered in record time and my portfolio didn't just bounce back; it multiplied.

That was the moment I truly understood "Aapda Me Avsar". Reflecting on my journey, I wrote a letter to myself in *My Investment diary:*

My Investment Diary

Today, I reviewed the stocks I reinvested in, back in 2021 and noticed how they have skyrocketed. It's now clear to me that panic selling does more damage than the market crash itself.

By staying calm and holding my position, I turned a market downturn into a real profit opportunity.

Debit: "A valuable lesson in keeping calm and recognising opportunities during in a market downturn"
Credit: "Profits from undervalued stocks acquired during the crisis"
(Net balance: A confident investor with a stronger conviction that crises can turn into opportunities if they are approached with patience and clarity)

09 Aug 2024
(Friday)

Opportunities do not arrive with dazzling banners; they often come disguised as chaos, catastrophe, and fear. Those who have the clarity to recognize these opportunities and the courage to act are the ones who reap the greatest benefits.

Just like shopping, in investing, you find the best deals when no one else is looking for them. So, the next time the market crashes and everyone panics, remember this:

- Panic is temporary. Value is permanent.
- Fear is loud, but opportunity whispers.
- When there's bloodbath on Dalal Street, smart money doesn't run; it buys.

Did You Know ?

During the 2008 financial crisis, when others were panicking, Warren Buffett invested $5 billion in Goldman Sachs and made a profit of over $3 billion within five years.

THE BOTTOM LINE

In the stock market, there will always be ups and downs, booms and busts, and bulls and bears. But history has shown us a simple truth. Disasters don't last forever, but the opportunities they create do.

Every crash feels like the end of the world, but what seems like an *Aapda* (catastrophe) today could turn into the greatest *Avsar* (opportunity) tomorrow. The trick? Keep a cool head when the market loses its mind.

However, it's important to emphasize that buying every stock that is in a downtrend is not advisable. Not every dip presents an opportunity and not every beaten-down stock is worth saving. The key is to buy strategically, which means making a list of fundamentally strong stocks you believe in and taking advantage of their lows to accumulate them at a discount. Think of it as a stock market sell-off; but instead of indiscriminately hoarding stocks just because they're cheap, focus on the ones which are fundamentally strong and you've been considering for a while.

The next time the market is gripped by panic, ask yourself, *"Are you the one who sells out of fear or the one quietly investing in great stocks at great prices?"* Because in investing, just like in life, the best rewards come to those who see what others do not.

The greater the difficulty, the more glory in surmounting it.

- Epictetus
(Greek Stoic philosopher)

MUTUAL FUND SAHI HAI?

Have you ever walked into a buffet, piled your plate high with food, and then realized that half of it wasn't that great?

It was one of those classic Friday nights. The end of a long workweek, a group of hungry friends, and an appetite that could rival a Bollywood hero's thirst for revenge. With growling stomachs, we entered a lively, bustling restaurant and skimmed the menu like stock analysts reviewing balance sheets. The problem? Everything looked tempting.

Paneer Tikka? Sounds delicious. *Biryani?* Always a winner. *Pasta?* An unexpected contender but worth a try! And then there was the humble but reliable *Dal Makhani,* the equivalent of a blue-chip stock. Faced with this paradox of choice, I did what any wise person would do: I asked the waiter, *"Do you have a platter?"*

He replied, *"Yes, sir. Which platter would you like?"*

Wait, what? I had expected a magical, all-inclusive solution that would allow me to enjoy a bit of everything without overthinking. But no, I was now faced with even more choices — the *Tandoori* platter, the South Indian platter, the

Continental platter; each promising a unique culinary journey. My stomach may have been empty, but my decision fatigue was at an all-time high.

To make matters worse, my friends had already made up their minds and were giving me impatient *"jaldi kar yaar"* looks. The pressure was mounting. My mind was racing, should I play it safe and choose something familiar, or take a risk and try something new? Should I go for variety or concentrate on one cuisine? Each option had its pros and cons and the more I thought about it, the harder the decision became.

I turned to the waiter for help. *"What can you recommend?"* His answer? A vague, non-committal, *"Sir, sab sahi hai!"* That was no help. I sighed, made a choice, picked one, and hoped for the best.

As we enjoyed our meal that night, I couldn't help but wonder why something as simple as ordering a meal had to be so complicated. When there are too many options and too little clarity, even a simple decision can feel like a high-stakes game.

Little did I know that this would not be the last time I was confronted with this dilemma and it wouldn't always be about food.

MARKET LENS

As I sat there staring at my platter, I realized that investing in Mutual Funds is just like choosing a meal at a restaurant.

You want a bit of everything — diversification, security, and returns. But if you pick blindly without knowing what's on the plate, you might walk away disappointed. Just as not all platters are created equal, some are packed with flavour, while others are just bland carbs. Similarly, not all mutual funds suit everyone.

The Mutual Fund industry has brilliantly marketed itself as a foolproof form of investment. The catchy *Mutual Fund Sahi Hai* campaign has convinced lakhs of people to enter the market without truly understanding what they are getting into. But here's the unpleasant truth — *Mutual Funds are not a one-size-fits-all solution!*

Let's step back and examine the challenges with Mutual Funds. If Mutual Funds are like a grand Indian *thali,* direct stock investing is more like ordering the chef's special *à la carte*, tailored precisely to your taste. While Mutual Funds may seem straightforward, they come with a complex web of fees, regulations, and restrictions. Here are the key issues:

- Over-diversification: Mutual funds typically hold 50 to 100 stocks. As a result, even the best-performing stocks barely move the needle. It's like going to a buffet and taking a spoonful of everything; you end up full but not truly satisfied by any one dish.
- Hidden costs: *Entry loads*[31], *exit loads*[32], *expense ratios*[33], and fund management fees quietly nibble away at your returns. It's like ordering biryani and then realising that raita and

[31] Entry load is a fee charged when an investor buys into a mutual fund or investment scheme, typically used to cover administrative costs.

[32] Exit load is a fee charged when an investor redeems or sells their mutual fund units before a specified period, meant to discourage early withdrawals.

[33] Expense ratio is the fee charged by a mutual fund, expressed as a percentage of the fund's assets. It covers management and operational costs. A higher expense ratio can significantly eat into an investor's returns over the long term.

salad cost extra. These charges may seem small, but over time, they can significantly reduce your long-term wealth.

- Fund mandates: A fund manager can't always act on great ideas. If a large-cap fund manager spots a winning mid-cap stock, they aren't allowed to invest. It's like craving Chinese food and being told, *"Sorry, we only serve South Indian"*.
- Lack of control during market extremes: Mutual funds are required to stay invested, even when markets are overheated. Direct stock investors can shift to cash, gold, or bonds when things get risky. Mutual fund managers, however, don't have that flexibility. Their money stays exposed whether they like it or not.

Wait a minute! Isn't diversification the key to smart investing? As discussed in the chapter *The 3-Plate Portfolio*, diversification is essential. But let's be clear — while diversification is crucial, Mutual Funds are not always the best solution.

Mutual Funds promise controlled diversification but often fall short and become inefficient. Instead of carefully selecting 10 to 15 high-quality stocks, like a well-planned buffet, they include 50 to 100 stocks, diluting the impact of their top performers.

If you still firmly believe that *Mutual Fund Sahi Hai*, let's examine some hard-hitting facts that might make you rethink. Are Mutual Funds truly beating the market? According to an August 2024 report in The Economic Times, titled "63% equity mutual funds fail to beat benchmarks in 3 years":

- 63% of equity funds have failed to outperform their benchmarks over the last three years.

- Only 78 out of 213 funds have outperformed their index, meaning nearly two-thirds of actively managed funds have disappointed investors.
- Small-cap and *flexi-cap*[34] funds have been the worst performers, proving that even aggressive funds do not always outperform direct stock picking.

So, if Mutual Funds are actively managed, why do so many perform poorly? A strong marketing campaign doesn't necessarily make them the right choice for everyone.

Now, let's revisit the idea of diversification. We all agree that diversification is important, but to what extent? I personally believe it's often discussed too broadly, without diving into the nuances. Warren Buffett famously said, *"Diversification is protection against ignorance"*. This means the extent to which an investor diversifies depends on their knowledge and ability to analyze stocks.

- For *"know-nothing"* investors, those with little knowledge or experience, broad diversification is a reliable way to reduce risk. It's similar to playing defensively in cricket, ensuring you stay in the game rather than getting out too early.
- For *"know-something"* investors, those with expertise to analyze companies thoroughly, a carefully selected set of high-quality stocks can lead to better results, much like confidently striking a well-timed six over the bowler's head.

While diversification helps manage risk, a well-structured portfolio strengthens confidence. The key is knowing when

[34] Flexi-cap fund is a type of mutual fund that invests in stocks across large, mid, and small-cap companies, with flexibility to adjust the allocation based on market conditions.

broad diversification is necessary and when a more refined approach can be more effective.

Did You Know ?

Warren Buffett typically maintains a portfolio of carefully selected stocks. For decades, over 70% of Berkshire Hathaway's investments have been focused on just five key stocks, including Apple, Bank of America, and Coca-Cola.

FROM MY JOURNEY

If I had received a rupee every time someone told me, *Mutual Fund Sahi Hai,* I would have enough money to start the "Grover Mutual Fund". Like many investors, I was attracted to the Mutual Fund universe with the promise of expert management, steady returns, and stress-free investing.

Back when I was a beginner in the stock market, i.e., eager, optimistic, and a bit overconfident; I jumped onto the Mutual Fund bandwagon without conducting proper research. A friend, whom I trusted more than a Wi-Fi connection during a live sports match, swore by a Blue-chip Fund he had invested in. His reasoning? *"It's managed by experts".* That was all the conviction I needed. Without a second thought, I clicked "Invest Now" in my app and officially became a Mutual Fund investor.

Everything seemed great in the first year. My money was growing, albeit slowly, but still. I already had big plans for my profits (not for retirement, but for a trip abroad and a fancy cell phone upgrade). Then reality hit.

After a few years, my Blue-chip Fund underperformed compared to the index. I reviewed the fund's holdings and found it stuffed with large-cap stocks that moved at the speed of a 1990s internet connection. Meanwhile, the broader market was rising and my direct stock investments were outperforming this expert-managed fund.

At this point, I realized I had blindly followed the Mutual Fund hype without understanding what I was getting myself into. It was like ordering a fancy platter without checking the ingredients. I expected *biryani* but got *khichdi* instead (no khichdi lover was harmed!). Here's an excerpt from *My Investment Diary:*

My Investment Diary

Today, I finally redeemed my very first investment in a Mutual Fund, with a disappointing return that barely outpaced inflation. What I thought was a foolproof investment turned out to be an expensive lesson in due diligence. I assumed that 'expert management' would automatically lead to better returns, but in reality, blindly trusting a fund is no better than blindly picking stocks.

Debit: "Missed potential for higher returns due to over-reliance on convenience"

Credit: "A lesson on the myth that Mutual Funds always deliver high returns"

(Net balance: A wiser investor who understands that 'Mutual Fund Sahi Hai' but only if carefully selected)

09 Sep 2019
(Monday)

That was the moment I experienced my Mutual Fund awakening. I stopped thinking of Mutual Funds as a shortcut to investing. I restructured my portfolio to focus on a mix of direct stock investments and carefully selected Mutual Funds, I came to terms with the fact that *Mutual Fund Sahi Hai,* but only if you choose wisely.

THE BOTTOM LINE

There's no denying that Mutual Funds are a good investment tool, but that's the keyword — a tool. They offer convenience, diversification, and professional management (or at least they claim to), but they're not a magic wand that guarantees wealth.

So, what's the real mantra here? Don't treat Mutual Funds as the ultimate solution to your stock market journey. Think of them as pre-packaged stock baskets with built-in diversification. They have their own set of limitations and it's your responsibility to research and choose the ones that actually align with your needs.

And while diversification remains a key principle of smart investing, Mutual Funds are not always the best way to achieve it. Here are a few pointers to keep in mind:

☑ Don't just invest in Mutual Funds. Invest in the RIGHT Mutual Funds.

☑ Understand your financial goals before picking a fund.

☑ Look beyond returns. Be aware of the costs, restrictions, and hidden clauses.

Investing without research is speculation. Investing with knowledge is the first step toward building wealth.

So, the next time someone says, *"Mutual Fund Sahi Hai"*, just smile and reply, *"Maybe. Let me figure out which one is 'Sahi' for me"*.

A ship in harbor is safe, but that is not what ships are built for.

- John A. Shedd
(American author)

THE 'RAPID' FORMULA

Have you ever resisted something with all your might, only to realize later that it would have been wiser to let it happen?

A few years ago, my friends and I took a trip to Rishikesh, the *"Yoga Capital"* of the World. But let's be honest, we weren't there to meditate or find inner peace. We were there for river rafting, the ultimate adrenaline rush on the Ganga. The rafting routes in Rishikesh vary in length, ranging from an easy 12 km to an extreme 30 km. In our overconfidence (and slight stupidity), we naturally signed up for the longest route, 30 km from *Kaudiyala* to *NIM Beach.*

The trip began peacefully, with breathtaking views of the mountains and the occasional playful lapping of the water. Our rafting guide, a man with a monk-like patience, encouraged us to try stunts, such as, standing on the edge, jumping into the river, and even flipping the raft (which we politely declined). It was all great fun until he suddenly screamed, *"Big rapid ahead! Sit still and go with the flow!"*

If you're not familiar with rafting, let me explain. Rapids are the river's version of a roller coaster; except there's no seatbelt and the water is actively trying to shake you off. Before I could process what was happening, we hit "The Wall", one of the most notorious rapids in Rishikesh, where 9 out of 10 rafts flip over. Our raft shook violently and spun us around like laundry in a washing machine. Panic spread. The temptation to jump off was great, but our guide kept shouting, *"Don't fight it! Go with the flow!"*

At first, we struggled against the current, fighting to regain control. But as we stopped resisting and let ourselves move with the river, something changed. That's when it clicked. The more we tried to resist the water, the worse it got. Yet as we adapted to the rhythm of the river, we glided through and even survived "The Wall".

Little did I know that this rafting lesson would turn out to be one of the most valuable investment lessons of my life. Just like the river, the stock market has its own flow and knowing when to go with it can make all the difference.

MARKET LENS

Let's transfer this rafting experience to the stock market. Just as the raft navigated through the waves, your portfolio must move with the market's natural movements. The stock market has its own dynamics and resisting it, whether out of fear or overconfidence, can lead to disastrous results, much like trying to row against the current in a raging rapid.

Think of the "raft" as your stock and the "river" as the market. You may row calmly, make calculated moves, and feel that you have everything under control. But when a rapid (or a sudden market momentum) occurs, it's best not to panic and jump out, but to stay on course and navigate with the flow.

Remember how our rafting instructor warned us not to leave the raft at "The Wall"? The same rule applies to investing, don't make impulsive decisions in the middle of a market storm. I'm not saying you should stay invested, no matter what, but rather that you shouldn't panic and make impulsive decisions.

In the stock market, momentum is often driven by strong forces, such as, liquidity, global events, or thematic trends. Post COVID-19, Indian markets witnessed a liquidity-driven rally, with unstoppable fund inflows pushing stocks higher and throwing traditional valuation logic out the window (faster than aunties do while bargaining in Sarojini Nagar). When you see sustained buying volumes and strong momentum, it's often a signal to go with the flow instead of heroically trying to swim against the tide.

Just to be clear, this doesn't mean you should go into Bollywood hero mode and blindly follow the trend without thinking. But it also doesn't mean you should play the rebellious investor for no reason. If your stock is rising steadily and has exceeded your expectations of fair value, instead of selling in panic, set a trailing stop loss[35], and let the momentum take its course.

What is a trailing stop loss[36]? Think of it like a seatbelt for your investment, it protects you without interrupting your journey. Let's say you buy a stock at ₹1,000 and set a trailing stop loss of 10%. Initially, the stop loss would be ₹900. If the stock rises to ₹1,200, the stop loss is adjusted to ₹1,080 (10% below ₹1,200). This way, you protect your profits while still riding

---

[35] Stop loss is an order placed with a broker to sell a security when it reaches a specific price to limit potential losses.

[36] Trailing stop loss is a stop-loss order that automatically adjusts to follow a stock's upward movement, locking in gains while limiting potential losses.

the wave. In short, you don't jump off the bus too early, but you ensure that you don't get stuck on the bus when it crashes.

Betting against the flow, believing that you can outsmart the market by catching the perfect dip or peak, often backfires. More often than not, investors find themselves in the same position I was in, when my raft was tossed back and forth in the rapids; confused, soaked, and regretful of my decisions.

Sometimes it's better to let the market settle down before taking the next step. Investing is not about fighting every current; it's about knowing when to paddle, when to hold still, and when to take the momentum.

Did You Know ?

Why do trends last longer than they should? Behavioral and emotional biases such as herd mentality, liquidity, and FOMO fuel them. Trends persist as long as people keep chasing them.

FROM MY JOURNEY

Let me share a lesson I learned the hard way. In March 2020, the COVID-19 outbreak triggered a market crash, causing the NIFTY to plunge over 30%, falling from 12,000 to around 8,000. My portfolio, which contained mid-cap and small-cap stocks, was hit even harder, losing over 40% of its value. However, by May 2020, the market had recovered. By June, the NIFTY rose back to 10,000+ and for the first time in months, I felt a glimmer of hope.

Despite this recovery, the environment remained chaotic. COVID cases were on a rise, speculation was rampant, and uncertainty was high. During this time, I came across a YouTube video by a self-proclaimed market guru who confidently predicted that the NIFTY would fall further to 7,700. His analysis, filled with historical charts and technical jargon, made me doubt my own judgment. Fear began to spread. This so-called expert who later became an internet meme known as *"7700 Wale Uncle"*, was convinced that another market collapse was inevitable.

Despite clear signs of market momentum, I let fear prevail over my logic. I panicked and sold a large part of my portfolio at a loss, believing I could re-enter the market at 7,700. However, that magic number never came. Instead, the NIFTY rose above 11,000, then above 12,000, eventually surpassing pre-COVID levels to cross 14,000 by December 2020. While others benefitted from the recovery, I found myself watching from the sidelines, annoyed that I had exited at the wrong time.

It was a humbling realization; I had been resisting the flow of the market instead of riding with it. Eventually, I overcame my fear-driven paralysis and re-entered the market in 2021, but by then, I had already missed out on significant opportunities. Many of the stocks I originally held had doubled or even tripled. Here's an excerpt from *My Investment Diary:*

My Investment Diary

Today, I reviewed my old investment records and saw my panicked sell-off from March 2020. The stocks I sold have doubled, tripled, or increased even more. That moment of fear, that one impulsive decision, cost me returns that I will never recoup. The market recovered, but I was too busy looking for reasons to doubt it.

Debit: "Lost potential gains by resisting market momentum"
Credit: "A lesson in embracing market trends instead of fighting them"
(Net balance: A more disciplined investor who understands that sometimes it's wiser to go with the flow rather than resist it)

21 Jun 2021
(Monday)

I have managed to rebuild my portfolio, but the experience taught me an important lesson. If the market is moving in one direction with strong momentum, don't overthink it and don't fight it. Let yourself go with the flow; otherwise, you could miss out on valuable opportunities.

THE BOTTOM LINE

Resisting strong market momentum is like paddling upstream, you waste energy, achieve nothing, and ultimately fall behind. Successful investing isn't about fighting every current, but about mastering the art of navigation.

When the market moves decisively, whether up or down, blind resistance leads to costly mistakes and missed opportunities. Fear-driven reactions and flawed logic have derailed countless investors, while those who understand momentum position themselves strategically to ride the wave.

This is not about mindlessly following the herd or ignoring risk. Momentum is a force to be respected, not blindly chased. Smart investors know that it's not about catching every wave but recognizing the ones worth riding. The biggest investing mistakes come from panic selling at the wrong time or clinging to bad positions out of stubbornness.

Instead, align with the trend, assess the momentum, and adjust accordingly. If a stock surpasses your fair value expectations, don't impulsively liquidate your holdings. Set a trailing stop loss, secure your profits, and stay engaged in the game

Like rafting, true mastery lies in understanding when to move with the current and when to take control. The market operates on its own rhythm and the investors who succeed are those who recognize how and when to navigate it effectively.

You don't win by resisting the market. You win by mastering its rhythm and making it work for you.

Do not resist life's flow: what you resist, persists.

- Carl Jung
(Swiss psychiatrist)

RISK AVERSE OR LOSS AVERSE?

What scares you more — the possibility of risk or the reality of loss? This distinction is the key to mastering your finances.

In 2017, during my first year in the corporate world after qualifying as a Chartered Accountant, I shared an apartment in Gurgaon with a colleague who later became a close friend. At the time, fantasy sports apps were booming, with *Dream11* leading the way for cricket fans. Being a die-hard cricket enthusiast (and still one today, though those were my most passionate fan years), I would eagerly create my *Dream11* fantasy teams for every IPL match.

Sometimes I won small amounts and sometimes I lost. However, I was always prepared to take risks and stuck to my rule: *"I only bet what I could afford to lose"*

Even when things didn't go my way, I stayed calm because I knew that risk was part of the game. Then, a moment arrived when I hit the jackpot, a big win that made me grin like a kid who found an extra chocolate bar in his lunchbox. Excited, I shared the news with my friend.

His reaction? Pure enthusiasm. His eyes lit up like *Diwali diyas.*

He was a cricket fan too but had never ventured into fantasy sports before. Eager to try it out, he asked me to explain the rules. I happily guided him through the app, helped him create his first team, and pointed out the risks. His response?

"Dude, I got it. I'm cool with losing a little bit".

When I heard *"Dude"*, *"got it"*, and *"cool"* in the same sentence, I was convinced he understood the game. The next day, I discovered he had bet ₹20,000, half his monthly salary, on a single match. He called himself a risk-taker and assured me he was fine with it. I was assured he fully understood the risks involved.

Oh, how wrong I was.

As his team's performance took a nosedive, his calm demeanour vanished. He screamed at the TV, paced back and forth, and prayed for a miraculous turnaround. The drama was nothing short of a Bollywood climax, ending in a heartbreak. He lost the entire ₹20,000.

Then, with the solemnity of *"Bhishma Pitamah"*, he swore never to play fantasy sports again. The drama was real, but so was the lesson.

MARKET LENS

This story about my friend's dramatic loss highlights an important distinction in the world of investing — the difference between *risk aversion*[37] and *loss aversion*[38]. They may

---

[37] Risk aversion is the tendency of an investor to prefer lower-risk options, even if they offer lower returns. A risk-averse person prioritizes safety of principal over potential high gains.

[38] Loss aversion is a behavioural finance concept describing how people feel the pain of losses more strongly than the pleasure of equivalent gains. Loss-averse investors might avoid selling a losing

sound similar, but they are as different as Test cricket and T20 regarding your behaviour in the stock market.

A risk-averse investor understands that losses are a natural part of the game. They take calculated risks, recognizing the possibility that things may not go as planned. When a loss occurs, they don't lose their nerve; they have mentally prepared for it and accept it as part of their journey. Imagine driving on a rainy day with your headlights on. You know visibility may be limited, but you're prepared for it.

In contrast, a loss-averse investor, like my friend, isn't fazed by the idea of risk but the moment a real loss hits, all composure vanishes. It's not risk they fear, it's the pain of losing that truly unsettles them.

Panic sets in, irrational decisions follow, and instead of cutting their losses, they cling to hope as if it were their last lifeline in *"Kaun Banega Crorepati"*.

They fear not only losing money, but also what that loss means — failure, regret, and shattered trust.

Many Indian investors fall precisely into the category of "loss averse but not risk averse". This behaviour is deeply cultural, rooted in how we, as a society, view failure and pride. For many, booking a loss feels like admitting defeat, a blow to one's self-image. Instead of exiting early and moving on, they cling to underperforming stocks, hoping for a miraculous Bollywood-style comeback that almost never arrives.

The script usually goes like this, *"Agar thoda aur ruk gaye, toh sab theek ho jayega"* (if I just hang on a little longer, everything

---

stock (or take other irrational actions) just to avoid realizing a loss.

will be fine). But instead of recovering, they watch their capital shrink further, as if waiting for a train that never arrives.

Investors become fixated on avoiding losses at all costs, even if it means missing out on valuable growth opportunities. While these habits are understandable, they can also be harmful if not recognized and addressed.

The key to overcoming this behaviour is to understand your risk appetite. Most investors confuse their capacity to take risks with their ability to absorb losses.

When these two factors don't align, poor investment decisions are the result. You may take risks believing you're prepared, but when losses occur, you realize that you're not emotionally able to handle them. Therefore, it's important to differentiate between these two aspects and manage both effectively.

FROM MY JOURNEY

Back in 2017, I believed I had mastered the stock market. Unlike those nervous, conservative investors who stick to fixed deposits and mutual funds, I was ready to take risks. In fact, I actively sought them out. After reading numerous books and watching interviews with legendary investors, I was convinced that high returns require high risk.

So, I confidently built up a "high conviction" portfolio. I didn't choose boring index funds; rather, I selected stocks that I believed had the potential to multiply in value. Initially, this strategy worked wonderfully.

My stocks skyrocketed, my portfolio looked like a dream, and I even started giving investment advice to my friends, spouting phrases like *"you have to think long-term"* and *"volatility is just noise"*.

Then came a market correction, a sharp one. Within a few weeks, my high-flying portfolio dropped by 15%.

At first, I shrugged it off, convinced that stocks don't rise in a straight line. *"This is only temporary"*, I told myself. But then the situation worsened,15% became 20%, then 25%.

Suddenly, my rational approach to investing vanished. Every morning, I woke up, checked my portfolio, and felt a wave of panic as I saw the deep red numbers.

"Maybe I should sell some stocks and buy them back later at a lower price?"

"What if the market crash continues? I can't afford to lose anymore!"

"What if these companies never recover?"

Eventually, I couldn't take it anymore. My confidence turned into pure fear. Convincing myself I was being practical; I decided to exit most of my positions before my losses grew any bigger. I sighed with relief; the fear was finally over.

And then? The market recovered.

Within six months, the same stocks I had sold at a loss of 20-25% had fully recovered and even surpassed their previous values. Had I simply held onto my investments and done nothing, my portfolio would have been in even better shape than before.

That experience marked a major turning point for me. I wasn't afraid of risk. I had willingly invested in stocks known for high volatility.

The real issue wasn't my willingness to take risks; it was my inability to tolerate temporary losses in my portfolio. I noted the following lesson in *My Investment Diary*:

> ***My Investment Diary***
>
> Today, I revisited my 2017 trades and recognised a clear pattern. I wasn't afraid of making risky investments; I was afraid of seeing losses on my screen. The moment my portfolio turned red, I let emotions guide me instead of logic. Instead of trusting my research, I exited trades too early, only to watch the same stocks rise and succeed later.
>
> Debit: "Missed opportunities due to emotional decisions"
> Credit: "A valuable lesson on the difference between prudent risk-taking and emotional reactions to loss"
> (Net balance: A more disciplined investor who understands that temporary setbacks are a natural part of long-term success)
>
> **15 Dec 2017**
> **(Friday)**

I was loss-averse, not risk-averse. Taking risks was never an issue for me. I was even willing to invest in high-growth stocks with *high volatility*[39]. However, when I saw that the numbers turned red, I panicked. The thought of losing money even on paper, was overwhelming, despite knowing that these stocks would fluctuate.

[39] High volatility is defined as the degree of variation in an asset's price over time. High volatility means the price swings widely (higher risk), while low volatility means the price is relatively stable. In markets, volatility is often used as a measure of risk or uncertainty.

This experience has changed the way I invest. Today, I know that temporary losses in the stock market are inevitable; however, real losses become certain if you panic and sell.

Now, when I see my portfolio in the red, I take a deep breath, remember 2017, and do what I should have done back then — *Nothing!*

One important lesson I've learned is that the market will test you. The real question is, *"Can you handle the red without running away?"* Because if you can, those who endure will ultimately be rewarded.

Pro Tip

Set a "panic threshold" before investing, such as a 30% drop, and document why it would trigger action. When panic sets in, refer to this rule as a safeguard. Calm decisions often outperform those made in chaos.

THE BOTTOM LINE

The stock market is filled with ups and downs and it's important that you learn how to control your emotions. Don't let them cloud your judgment when making investment decisions.

Just as Kabir Singh must control his temper, you must control your emotions when it comes to investing. Otherwise, you might end up yelling at the screen, *"NIFTY! NIFTY!"* in a dramatic fashion like Kabir Singh shouting *"Preeti! Preeti!"* (I hope you're reading this in his voice; full of drama!).

Emotional decisions often lead to costly mistakes. Whether you refuse to sell a stock at a loss out of fear or cling to the hope that a bad investment will miraculously recover, it's a recipe for disaster. Avoid following the crowd and develop your own rational approach.

It is not the things themselves that disturb men, but their judgments about these things.

- Epictetus
(Greek Stoic philosopher)

15 TUG OF WAR: GREED VS. FEAR

Have you ever fallen for the 'limited time offer' trap and ended up buying things you never planned to?

That day at *Big Bazaar* felt like a war zone. Carts crashing. Aunties elbowing. Kids wailing over chocolates. The air was thick with the smell of freshly baked cookies. Banners screamed *"Buy 2 Get 1 Free!"* and suddenly, everything in the store felt essential.

Logic? Not even close. Self-control? Absolutely non-existent. I ended up grabbing a set of mixing bowls (did I need them? Absolutely not), a pack of towels (because you can never have enough), and, to top it all off, a foot massager (seriously, why?). An item I had never even considered before now felt like an essential part of my life, all thanks to the sale.

By the time I got home, the shopping madness had worn off, leaving me with a grim realization. What the hell just happened? Did I suddenly develop a passion for foot massages? And why did I buy so many mixing bowls as if I were starting a catering business?

The answer was simple, greed had hijacked my brain. The excitement of a "great deal" overwhelmed my thinking and convinced me that I needed things I didn't actually need. It was the classic "buy now, think later" trap. A trap that retailers love and shoppers later regret. And if you think this phenomenon is limited to *Big Bazaar* sales, think again.

MARKET LENS

The exact same psychological tug-of-war plays out every day in the stock market, where greed and fear wrestle for control. The moment you let emotions take over, you stop investing and start reacting. And that shift can be the difference between a big win and a complete loss.

One moment, investors are euphoric, convinced that stock prices will rise forever. The next, they're in panic mode, selling everything as if the world is ending. It's Greed (a.k.a. fear of missing out) versus Fear (a.k.a. fear of losing everything) — a battle that never truly ends.

When the markets soar, greed whispers, *"This time it's different, keep buying"*. Investors toss caution aside, believing that stocks will never fall. The real estate bubble of 2008? The dot-com craze? Surely those were different times! Spoiler alert: they weren't.

However, when the markets collapse, fear dominates. Investors rush to sell because they are convinced that every stock is doomed. It doesn't matter how strong a company is; when the herd runs, they run too. Remember March 2020? Investors dumped stocks as if they were ticking time bombs, only to see the markets rebound faster than a Bollywood hero in a fight scene.

The truth? Neither extreme is rational. Markets will always have cycles. Stock prices will rise and fall and the biggest mistake investors make is getting swept in the emotional rollercoaster of greed and fear.

The stock market doesn't communicate verbally, but it plays its own version of *"Dumb Charades"*. The problem? Most investors misinterpret the clues. If you can't recognize whether the market is acting out of "greed" or "fear", you risk chasing overvalued stocks or selling in a panic. Let's decode the game. Here's what greed and fear *sound* like:

When the market lives out "GREED"

- Stocks are soaring. WhatsApp explode with "multi-bagger alert" messages, and your neighbour, who just learned about SIPs, is suddenly giving stock tips.
- IPOs are oversubscribed like a free buffet. Every company, regardless of stability, gets premium valuations as if fundamentals no longer matter.
- Logic? That's gone on vacation. People are buying anything with a ticker, convinced that *"this time it's different"*.

What should you do? Don't be the last one dancing when the music stops. Book profits, rebalance your portfolio, and don't chase FOMO rallies. Remember, *"Profit wahi jo haath mein aaye"* (only profit that counts is the one you take home).

When the market lives out "FEAR"

- Business news channels resemble doomsday preppers, screaming "MARKET CRASH! INVESTORS IN PANIC!"
- The same people who previously bought stocks blindly are now selling in panic, convinced that the market will never recover.
- Suddenly, value stocks are available at a discount, but no one wants to touch them as they think it's the "endgame" for market.

What should you do? Now is the time to put on your research hat and go on a shopping spree. When everyone is fearful, valuations become attractive. But don't just buy everything, focus on quality stocks with strong fundamentals.

Did You Know ?

Studies in behavioural economics show that investors experience the pain of losses twice as intensely as the joy of equivalent gains. This is why, at the first sign of trouble, they sell in panic yet hesitate to buy even in a booming market.

The smartest investors are the ones who observe, interpret correctly, and act with logic. Greed and fear will always be part of the market, but the key is to recognise these emotions and not let them drive your decisions.

After all, the stock market isn't about making perfect predictions. It's about staying in the game long enough to win.

FROM MY JOURNEY

I have had my share of battles with greed and fear. As I write this in October 2024, the Indian stock market seems to be in an unstoppable bull run. Market indices have recently hit lifetime highs, i.e., the NIFTY has crossed the 26,000 mark and the SENSEX has surged past the 85,000 as of September 2024, the numbers that would have seemed like fantasy just a few years ago. From the local *Paanwala* to the self-proclaimed YouTube market gurus, everyone suddenly has a price target and the consensus seems to be that stocks can only rise.

It's a party and everyone is invited. The market has nearly tripled since its low in 2020 and whispers of NIFTY rising to 30,000, 40,000 or even 50,000 are circulating like Bollywood plot twists. The excitement is contagious, just like a flash sale where everyone scrambles to grab a deal before it's over.

However, history has taught me one thing. When greed reaches its peak, caution is necessary. I've seen this movie before (and it's certainly not the feel-good story). The valuations are stretched and the market seems to defy gravity. It reminds me of "*Mithun Da*" dodging bullets and hiding behind a bicycle; it looks cool, but we all know it won't last forever. Markets don't just keep climbing without corrections.

Now, you should have a clear picture of how the force of "Greed" operates. Let's turn our focus to "Fear", the other extreme force driving the stock market.

This brings me back to March 2020 when the world came apart at the seams. The COVID-19 pandemic had sent shockwaves across the globe, causing the stock market to plummet. The NIFTY and SENSEX plummeted faster than a villain's loyal goon being tossed off a cliff in a Bollywood climax. March 23, 2020, was devastating. SENSEX lost over 13% in a single day and the NIFTY followed suit. Investors panicked, sold everything, and tried to escape the market like passengers jumping off the Titanic.

If I'm being completely honest, I was one of them. Amid the chaos, I panicked and sold a large chunk of my portfolio, gripped by the same fear I had promised myself to avoid. Watching the market collapse day after day felt like entering survival mode. It wasn't a rational decision; it was pure, naked fear.

But once the dust settled, I started to question my actions. Had I really made a rational decision or had I been overtaken by panic? In that moment of reflection, I realized my mistake. In early 2021, I changed my approach, instead of fleeing, I began buying. That turned out to be one of the best decisions of my investment journey.

It felt like the stock market's version of *Flipkart Big Billion Days* or *Amazon Great Indian Festival,* but I wasn't buying gadgets; I was acquiring fundamentally strong stocks at massive discounts.

These two moments! The irrational greed of 2024 and the sheer panic of 2020 serve as a proof that the market is always in a tug-of-war between greed and fear. Those who can step back, detach from their emotions, and make rational decisions are the ones who ultimately succeed. Here's an excerpt from *My Investment Diary:*

> ***My Investment Diary***
>
> I reflect on two pivotal moments in my investment journey: March 2020 and October 2024. In March 2020, fear drove me to panic-sell my stocks. Now, in October 2024, greed is everywhere, tempting me to buy more. But this time, I am staying rational, focused on fundamentals, and not letting these forces dictate my decisions
>
> These experiences highlight the two dominant forces in the market: fear and greed. There will always be a constant tug-of-war between them, shaping investor behavior and market cycles.
>
> Debit: "Lost potential gains from missed opportunities"
> Credit: "A lesson on the power of rational and logical decisions"
> (Net balance: A calm investor who knows that lasting success comes from staying rational)
>
> **12 Oct 2024**
> **(Saturday)**

THE BOTTOM LINE

The stock market is not merely a numbers game; it is fundamentally a battle of emotions. At its core, it is a psychological tug-of-war between greed and fear. Those who master their emotions will emerge victorious in the end.

When greed gains the upper hand, logic often takes a back seat. Investors believe in endless rallies and are convinced that stocks can only go up. However, when fear dominates the market, even the best investment opportunities are ignored because panic blinds people to reality. The key to success? Recognize these emotions and ensure they don't dictate your decisions.

As Warren Buffett famously said, *"Be fearful when others are greedy and greedy when others are fearful"*. The market will continue to fluctuate between euphoria and despair, but the trick is to stay grounded while others float away, either on a cloud of overconfidence or a storm of panic.

By keeping your emotions under control, sticking to your strategy, and being the one who sees opportunities when others see a crisis, you will not only survive the market's ups and downs but thrive in them as well.

Life is a balance of holding on and letting go.

- Rumi
(Persian poet and Sufi mystic)

THINK BEYOND THE REARVIEW

Would you trust a 10-year-old map in a city where roads keep changing, new ones emerge, and old ones disappear?

Growing up, I was a die-hard WWE fan. Every Sunday, my friends and I would gather in front of the TV with snacks in hand and watch as our favourite wrestlers battled in the ring. It was more than just entertainment; it was a ritual, a religion, a way of life. Among all the wrestling legends, one name stood out above the rest: *The Undertaker,* the Deadman. His WrestleMania streak was legendary. Year after year, he remained undefeated on WWE's biggest stage. For us, the idea of *The Undertaker* losing a match was simply unimaginable.

As the years went by, nostalgia washed over me in 2014 when I met up with an old friend. We decided to watch a WWE event together. The excitement was high. It was WrestleMania and when the wrestlers entered the ring, I experienced a sense of *déjà vu. "Who do you think will win?"* my friend asked, flashing his familiar mischievous grin. *"The Undertaker, of course",* I replied without hesitation. *The Undertaker* had never lost at WrestleMania before. Why should this time be any different?

And then, it happened. *Brock Lesnar* pinned *The Undertaker.* One. Two. Three! The winning streak was over. Silence fell over the arena. The crowd didn't scream or cheer; they stood frozen, their faces reflecting a mixture of disbelief and existential crisis. This was not just another match; it was the moment when the impossible became reality.

It was a humbling experience that taught me that even legends like *The Undertaker* are not immune to change. The dynamics of wrestling had changed; new competitors had emerged, hungrier, and stronger than ever. No matter how dominant the past once was, the future always writes its own rules.

MARKET LENS

This lesson extends beyond wrestling; it applies significantly to the stock market. Just because a company has performed well in the past does not mean it will continue to do so in the future. Past performance is part of the story, not the whole story.

Investors, especially beginners, are often tempted by the glittering returns of the past. They look at the historical performance of a stock and assume it will continue to rise. It's like betting on *The Undertaker* because of his legendary WrestleMania streak.

Many investors fall into this trap, believing the future will reflect the past. But the stock market is as unpredictable as the weather in Mumbai during the monsoon; it can change suddenly in the blink of an eye. Relying only on past performance is like judging a book by its cover. While it's helpful to know where a company has been, but to really understand its future potential requires looking deeper, examining fundamentals, reviewing market trends, and assessing growth prospects.

> **Did You Know ?**
>
> The Japanese Nikkei index peaked in 1989, and it took more than 30 years to reach that level again. Previous highs do not always mean that things will rise again in the future.

Here's, a real-world example. Unitech, once a rising star in the Indian real estate boom, illustrates how past performance is no guarantee of future success. Between 2003 and 2008, the company's stock price skyrocketed from ₹0.3 to ₹500, generating a return of over 1,50,000 % as the Indian real estate market flourished. Investors were convinced that the company was unstoppable. However, the 2008 financial crisis brought a harsh reality. Rising debts, project delays, and regulatory hurdles caused the high-flyer to plummet. By 2013, Unitech's stocks had plummeted to around ₹35, erasing almost all its previous gains, a fall of over 95% from its peak.

Just because Unitech was the top-performing stock last year does not mean it will achieve the same success again. Market conditions change and factors such as new technologies, regulations, government policies, and competition all influence a company's future. Relying solely on past performance is like looking in a rearview mirror; useful, but not the whole picture.

The market is filled with stories of stocks that once soared to legendary heights, only to become cautionary tales. Here are a few examples that prove why relying solely on past performance can be misleading:

Example of "Once Legends, Now Lessons"

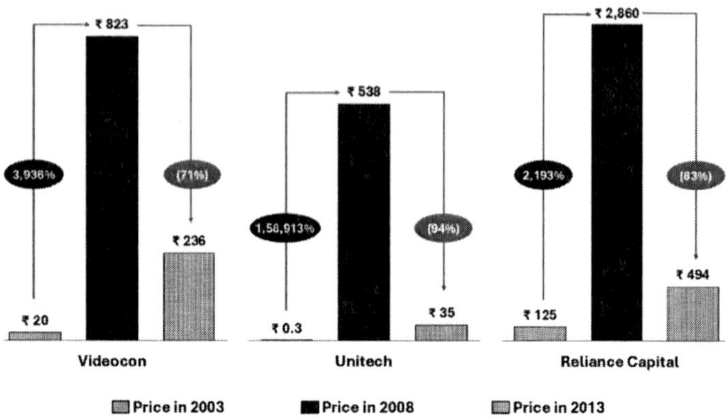

Instead of relying on past performance, consider where a company is headed by analysing the following factors:

- Match stock price growth with revenue trends. If the stock is surging while earnings stagnate, tread carefully.
- Assess market position. Is the company gaining ground or losing relevance? Adaptability is key.
- Gauge innovation. Leaders invest in R&D; laggards slash budgets and fall behind.
- Evaluate leadership. Has management steered through storms, or are they just riding the highs?

FROM MY JOURNEY

Let me share a story that highlights this lesson perfectly. A friend of mine was just starting his investment journey in 2017. He was particularly interested in Mutual Funds and like any newbie, wanted the highest possible returns. I suggested him to analyse the "Scheme Information Document (SID)" and "Key Information Memorandum (KIM)". I know *Sid* and *Kim* sound like names of distant relatives you only meet at weddings, but they are important documents that give detailed insights into the investments, risk profiles, and objectives of a Mutual Fund.

Did my friend analyze these factors? Of course not. Instead, he took the easy way out. He opened a financial app, sorted Mutual Funds by last year's performance, and chose the one with the highest return. It was a fund from the defence sector that had performed incredibly well last year. I warned him that past performance isn't everything, but he wasn't listening. Success can make people deaf to caution.

Fast forward one year. The market had achieved excellent returns overall, but my friend's portfolio had fallen by 10%. The high-flying defence sector fund he had chosen had underperformed, primarily due to political changes that negatively impacted the sector. He had fallen into the past performance trap.

This experience taught him the hard way that yesterday's hero may not be tomorrow's star. It's easy to be dazzled by numbers, but when investing, it's important to dig deeper. As I often say, two types of people rarely listen to advice — those who have won elections and those who have made money in the stock market. That same day, I decided to document the lesson, after all, it's always smarter to learn from others' mistakes rather than make them yourself. Here's an excerpt from *My Investment Diary:*

My Investment Diary

Today, I recorded a lesson, not from my own mistake but from that of a friend. He chose a Mutual Fund from the defence sector because he assumed that its past success would continue. Today, his portfolio is in the red. This experience brought home a simple truth: Markets change, and past performance is no guarantee of future gains.

Debit: "A lesson in prioritizing future potential over past performance"
Credit: "Avoided poor returns in the defence sector fund"
(Net balance: A smart investor focusing on the future instead of dwelling on the past)

06 Nov 2018
(Tuesday)

THE BOTTOM LINE

The market rewards those who evolve, not those who cling to past glories. Just like the legendary streak of *The Undertaker,* past victories can be deceptive. In the world of investing, you shouldn't be guided by historical performance alone. Of course, it's tempting to pounce on a stock or fund that has been successful in the past but remember — *"Past glory says nothing about future success"*.

The stock market is dynamic, constantly evolving and merciless to those who do not adapt. Strategies that worked yesterday may not be effective tomorrow. That's why smart investors don't just focus on glittering returns from the past; they analyze fundamentals, industry trends, and future potential.

Look to the past for guidance, not for shortcuts, stock tips, or ready-made picks. After all, the market is not just about where a company has been but about where it is headed.

The past is a place of reference, not a place of residence.

- Roy T. Bennett
(American author)

"N+1" SCENARIO

Have you ever made a plan that was so perfect that nothing could go wrong until it did?

I've always taken pride in being a master planner. The kind of person who has a plan, a backup plan, and a backup to the backup plan. Whether preparing for exams, planning a family vacation, or strategizing for a weekend cricket match, I had everything planned down to the last detail.

Flashback to 2015, I was well prepared for my CA final exams. I had rushed through CPT and IPCC, meticulously planned my three-year CA training (articleship), and created study plans so detailed that they made NASA's Mars mission look easy.

Everything went according to plan. I had foreseen every possible problem, had plans A, B and C ready, and felt as confident as a YouTube expert predicting a market crash in every thumbnail.

A month before my exams, I was hit by something unexpected — *Dengue!* Yes, you read that right. A mosquito-sized villain single-handedly thwarted my grand plan. I was suffering from high fevers, body aches, and a battered immune system, while my precious, foolproof planning lay in ruins. Suddenly, all my carefully crafted strategies seemed as useless as a stock tip from a Telegram group.

Somehow, I managed to drag myself into the exam hall because giving up was not part of my plan, but my brain felt like a crashed stock market, completely wiped out. I got through only two exams (in CA, we call them exemptions), which meant I had to retake the rest of the exams.

The master planner in me was humbled. A few months later, after endless cups of *chai,* intense study sessions, and a new perspective on failure, I finally passed my CA exam in May 2016. But the most important lesson I learned was not from the syllabus but from real life. No matter how well you plan and how many "N" number of scenarios you come up with, life always has an extra, unexpected twist, which I call "N+1" scenario.

MARKET LENS

If you think life is unpredictable, try predicting the stock market. It's like trying to predict the Indian monsoon, one moment the sun is shining, and the next you're knee-deep in water, wondering what went wrong.

Every investor, from beginners to billionaires, has tried to plan for every possible outcome. Yet the market always finds a way to introduce an "N+1" scenario; something no one saw coming.

Let's start with a legendary example of overconfidence meeting the unexpected — Bill Hwang and Archegos Capital.

This man was not just any fund manager; he managed tens of billions of dollars and made massive, highly leveraged bets on stocks like ViacomCBS. On paper, everything looked perfect. His strategy had been working for years and he was convinced he had mastered the game.

Then the "N+1" scenario struck. ViacomCBS stocks plummeted unexpectedly, triggering a chain reaction of margin calls. In just a few days, Archegos Capital collapsed, wiping out $20 billion (about 1.65 lakh crore). Yes, ₹1.65 lakh crore, gone quicker than cricket tickets for an India-Pakistan World Cup match.

What was the mistake? Overconfidence. Bill Hwang had planned everything, except for the one thing he never thought would happen. Turns out, markets don't care how prepared you think you are.

And this isn't just a global story. Indian investors have also learnt this lesson the hard way, often when they least expected it. Here are some classic market shocks that caught even the smartest investors off guard:

- **2008 financial crisis:** Everyone believed in "India decoupling" (meaning India would not be affected by the US financial mess). But it didn't work out that way. The Sensex plunged from 21,000 to 8,000.
- **COVID-19 market slump (March 2020):** The market was soaring, investors were celebrating, and then boom! A virus from Wuhan brought the global economy crashing down and the Sensex lost 38% within a month.
- **Adani Group Rout (2023):** Investors pounced on Adani stocks with unstoppable momentum until Hindenburg

Research published a report that wiped out investors' $150 billion (about ₹ 12.4 lakh crore).

Do you recognize a pattern? Every major market crisis has been triggered by an unexpected, unconsidered factor, the "N+1" scenario.

Planning is good, but flexibility is even better. In the stock market, as in life, it's not just an advantage to expect the unexpected; it's a survival strategy. So when you set up your investment strategy, always leave room for the "N+1" scenario, because sooner or later, the market will throw one at you.

Did You Know ?

Long-Term Capital Management (LTCM), a hedge fund run by Nobel Prize-winning economists, collapsed in 1998 after its "foolproof" financial model failed, resulting in a loss of $4.6 billion.

FROM MY JOURNEY

Speaking of overconfidence, let me share a lesson I learned the hard way with Infosys stock. Yes, I, the self-proclaimed master planner, fell straight into the market's favourite trap, *"I had it all figured out"*.

It was 2020 and by that time I had already faced significant losses while experimenting with *intraday trading*[40]. After some

[40] Intraday trading is defined as buying and selling financial instruments (like stocks) within the same trading day, aiming to profit from short-term price movements. All positions are closed by end of day to avoid overnight risk.

painful lessons (read: losses), I decided to focus on long-term investing.

But as they say, old habits die hard and in my case, bad habits die even harder. Infosys had just announced its quarterly results on Friday evening and immediately afterward, its stock shot up 5% in the U.S. stock market. Yes, you read that right; Infosys stocks are also traded on the New York Stock Exchange (NYSE) through a process called *ADR*[41] *(American Depository Receipts).*

I said to myself, *"This will surely surge on Monday in India!"* After all, if Infosys is rising in the U.S., it should open higher in India too, right?

The setup was perfect. "Right place, right time" or so I thought. Monday morning came and I was glued to my screen like a cricket fan watching the Super Over of the World Cup. To my surprise, Infosys opened flat. I saw it as my *Wolf of Wall Street* moment *(a.k.a. Dalal Street ka Bhediya)* and yelled, *"Got the perfect entry!"*

My confidence went into beast mode. I wasn't just dipping my toes in; I was going "all in". I made a massive bet on Infosys *call options*[42] with whatever spare cash I had in my account, convinced that I'd be on my way to Goa by the afternoon, funded by my trade profits. The plan was simple:

☑ Buy Infosys call options.

---

[41] ADR is a negotiable certificate issued by a U.S. bank representing shares of a foreign company. ADRs allow investors to trade international stocks on U.S. exchanges in U.S. dollars, simplifying investment in foreign companies.

[42] Call options is a type of derivative contract that gives the buyer the right (but not the obligation) to purchase a stock (or other asset) at a specified price (the strike price) before or on a specified expiration date. It's essentially a leveraged bet that the stock's price will rise.

☑ Watch the stock go up.

☑ Sell at a massive profit.

☑ Book a ticket to Goa and go to Baga Beach.

Simple plan, right? Wrong again. By Monday afternoon, instead of soaring, Infosys stocks crashed; not by 2% or 3%, but by a whole 10%! It felt like the market looked at me and said, *"Beta, ye market hai, yahaan sab chalta hai!"* (Kid, this is the stock market. Anything can happen here!).

My call options lost 90% of their value within a few hours. I sat there staring at my screen in disbelief. It was as if I was watching my hard-earned money vanish into thin air, faster than a friend who owes you money. In that moment, I couldn't understand what had happened. The stock was supposed to go up, not nosedive. Here is snapshot from my portfolio:

Name	Qty Long Term Qty	Avg Buy Price Buy Value	Avg Sell Price Sell Value	LTP Mkt. Value	Unrealized P&L	Realized P&L	Total P&L
INFY-OPT-29OCT2020-CE-1160-NSE	7,200.00	15.06 1,08,432.00	- -	- -		-1,08,432.00 (-100.00%)	-1,08,432.00 (-100.00%)

But why? I had considered everything… or at least, I thought I had. What I failed to account for were the silent predators of the market — the operators, a.k.a. the real sharks.

✦ They take the opposite bet.

✦ They push the stock down.

✦ They "eat" the call premiums.

The next day, Infosys rebounded and shot up by 15%, but by then, my money was already gone. The market had humbled me in the most brutal way. Here's an excerpt from *My Investment Diary:*

> ### *My Investment Diary*
>
> Today, I learned the hard way that no trade is ever guaranteed. I thought I had all the facts: strong earnings, a rising ADR, a clear trend. Yet, the market had other plans. I went "all in" and was sure I had everything under control. I ended up losing a sizable amount on that aggressive bet and learned the valuable lesson that you can't predict the market accurately, especially "when" a particular move will occur.
>
> Debit: "Substantial losses on Infosys call options"
> Credit: "A hard lesson in expecting the unexpected and never betting everything on a single trade"
> (Net balance: A wiser investor who understands that the market always has more surprises in store)
>
> **19 Oct 2020**
> **(Monday)**

I learned a valuable and expensive lesson. Never assume that the market will behave exactly as you expect it to. The moment you think you've cracked the code; the market will present an "N+1" scenario that turns your logic upside down.

THE BOTTOM LINE

The key to survival lies not only in anticipating all possible scenarios, but also in being flexible, adaptable, and humbly accepting that you won't always be right.

In investing, the only certainty is uncertainty. The best investors are not those who predict every move correctly; they are the ones who prepare for when things don't go as planned. That's where a few smart habits come in handy:

☑ **Diversify wisely:** Never bet everything on one outcome.

☑ **Hedge your risks:** Market loves to throw curveballs.

☑ **Keep liquidity ready:** Opportunities arise when chaos strikes.

Ultimately, no one can predict the market with absolute certainty. However, if you build your portfolio in a well-prepared and adaptable way, you stand the best chance of being successful, even if the unexpected happens.

Because in investing, as in life, there is always an "N+1" scenario waiting just around the corner.

The more you know, the more you know, you don't know.

- Aristotle
(Greek philosopher and polymath)

THE 'JOMO' INVESTOR

Have you ever regretted not doing something and wished you had a time machine to go back and do it?

As a child, nothing matched the thrill of slurping on a *"gola"*, that colourful icy delight also known as *"chuski"* or *"barf ka gola"*, depending on which corner of India you were in. These colourful, syrupy ice cubes were summer in a cup. But alas, those carefree days are behind me. With the concept of calories now part of my vocabulary and tooth sensitivity creeping into my life like an uninvited guest, I've had to say goodbye to my *"gola"* eating adventures.

Back then? I was an ice cream maximalist. One flavour was never enough. I still remember the day my dad said, *"Puttar, order what you want"*, and my brain lit up like a trader watching the Sensex go green.

Initially, I confidently chose mango flavour... a safe, classic choice. But then I discovered orange, with its tangy, citrusy deliciousness. How could I resist? So, I switched. Just as I was about to make my final decision, my eyes fell on Milk Pistachio, which was not only delicious but also healthy (after all, it had milk in it, right?). Without hesitation, I switched to Milk Pistachio, quicker than a politician switching parties before the elections.

Dad looked at me with the expression of a man reconsidering all his life decisions. When I realized that his patience was waning, I quickly assured him, *"Bas, last change!"*

But then I saw an ice cream sandwich. Two crunchy cookies hugged a scoop of ice cream like a warm, loving embrace. My eyes lit up like a Diwali advertisement promoting 90% off. This was it, the ultimate jackpot. I had to have it. After some emotional manipulation, light bargaining, (and of course some typical Punjabi style *"love taps"* from my dad), I finally got my ice cream sandwich.

And you know what? I didn't enjoy it. Instead of savouring the treat in my hands, I found myself wondering about what I had missed. Maybe mango would have been better? Maybe I should have stuck with orange? Instead of enjoying what I had, I regretted what I hadn't chosen.

Today, I realize that it wasn't just about ice cream; it was my first encounter with FOMO: Fear of Missing Out.

On the other hand, my elder brother was wired differently. While I battled choice paralysis, he always knew exactly what he wanted. He decided, even before we left the house, *"Orange gola"*. No distractions, no second thoughts. He ordered it, savoured every bite and left with no regrets. If he saw something else later, he would casually shrug his shoulders and say, *"Chal koi na, next time"*.

Meanwhile, I stood there eating my *gola,* but mentally, I was living in an alternative universe where I had made a different decision.

MARKET LENS

The ice cream chaos from my childhood? That's exactly what happens in the stock market; only we're juggling between hot stocks instead of flavours. You've probably heard this at family gatherings, office discussions or in WhatsApp investor groups:

"If you had bought Deepak Nitrite in 2017, you'd be a millionaire today!"

"XYZ stock has gone up 5x! I told you, but you didn't listen!"

Regret, panic, and the worst feeling when investing — FOMO. The moment you hear about a stock that has surged by 300% in six months, your brain creates a fantasy where you've invested in it and are now lying in the Maldives, sipping coconut water. Meanwhile, reality catches up. You didn't invest and you're left staring at your underperforming portfolio, wondering if you should dump everything to chase the next "sure thing".

This way of thinking is dangerous. Investing based on regret or hype is like ordering an ice cream just because someone else is eating it, without knowing if you even like that flavour.

The FOMO trap means that no one talks about the losers, i.e., hyped stocks that have crashed harder than a Bollywood debutante's career. For every stock that has doubled, there are ten others that have wiped out the fortune, but you rarely hear about them.

- Remember the hype surrounding Yes Bank in 2018? The "next big thing" in banking? Well, it was certainly big enough to wipe out 90% of investor wealth when reality caught up with it.

- What about Suzlon Energy? Once hailed as the next giant of renewable energy, the company has become a slow-motion disaster.
- And let's not forget Jet Airways, where investors held on until the company literally ran out of fuel, both financially and operationally.

The problem is that FOMO investors love to highlight past winners while conveniently ignoring disasters. No one talks about Yes Bank, Suzlon, or Jet Airways once they crash and burn.

Looking back, I realise my elder brother had it figured out long before I did. His calm *"Chal koi na, next time"* attitude was more than just maturity. It was what I now call JOMO[43] — *Joy of Missing Out.* Instead of viewing missed opportunities as failures, recognize them as a superpower. Here's a new way to look at it:

- **Missed investing in Bitcoin at $100?** No problem! You also missed buying Luna before it collapsed to zero? Even better.
- **Missed the rally in Deepak Nitrite?** No problem! You also avoided buying Zee Entertainment before it collapsed? That's a win!

Instead of dwelling on missed opportunities, train yourself to focus on what you have and where you can still create wealth.

[43] JOMO is a mindset opposite of FOMO, where an investor is content with not joining every market craze. It emphasizes satisfaction in sticking to one's own strategy and not worrying about missed opportunities – focusing instead on long-term goals and peace of mind.

The stock market is not a single meal; it's an all-you-can-eat buffet. When one dish is gone, another will follow.

FROM MY JOURNEY

In my early days as an investor, FOMO had a stranglehold grip on me tighter than a Monday morning traffic jam in Gurugram. If a stock had already doubled, I would still tell myself, *"Abhi bhi time hai, aur upar jayega!"* (It's not too late, it will go up further).

One of the most important lessons I learned was by observing experienced investors, people who had been in the market much longer than I had. They weren't glued to stock forums or anxiously following price movements every five minutes. Instead, they were calm, composed, and strangely content, even when they weren't doing anything.

I once asked an experienced investor about a stock that had risen by 200% in six months. *"Sir, did you invest in this stock?"*

He smiled and said, *"Nahi"*. Shocked, I asked, *"Don't you feel bad? I mean, look at the returns!"*

His answer? *"Beta, share bazaar ka buffet kabhi khatam nahi hota"* (Stock market always serves another opportunity, the buffet never really ends).

This one line changed my perspective. The market isn't a one-time offer where you either seize the opportunity or lose it forever. It's an all-you-can-eat buffet where there are always new dishes, some potentially better than the last. Slowly, I began to practice JOMO. Instead of chasing every *hot stock,* I focused on what made sense to me.

Let's take October 2024, the markets were on fire. Indices were hitting new highs and WhatsApp groups were flooded with messages like *"Once in lifetime opportunity. Now or never"*. A classic FOMO trap.

But instead of plunging, I took a step back. I booked the gains from 75% of my portfolio and shifted the funds into safer investments such as GILT funds and gold. It wasn't an easy decision; I knew some stocks could still go up, but I'd seen enough bubbles burst to know when it was time to play it safe.

And you know what? Now, in November 2024, when the markets corrected a little, the same people who had mocked my decision asked, *"Bro, what to do now? Shall we Hold or Sell?"*

Quick Hack

Before you buy a stock, ask yourself: Will I hold it with conviction if it falls by 20%? If you hesitate, it's FOMO driving your decision, not rational investment thinking.

That was the moment when I really understood the power of JOMO. Not every opportunity is meant for you. Missing out on the wrong things is just as important as investing in the right things. I opened *My Investment Diary* and wrote down this lesson:

My Investment Diary

Today I learnt that not doing anything can be a smart move too. The market was booming, everyone seemed in a rush to buy. But I stayed calm, booked some profits, and didn't give in to the noise.

Now that the market is correcting, I can see the value of patience. I'm not stressed or second-guessing. FOMO didn't win this time, and I'm better off for it.

Debit: "A lesson in finding value in the joy of missing out"
Credit: "A considerable amount of money secured by avoiding market hype"
(Net balance: A disciplined investor who knows that sometimes the best trade is the one not made)

21 Nov 2024
(Thursday)

Today, I no longer feel pressured to constantly invest in the market. I enjoy waiting for the right prices, taking profits when valuations seem inflated, and ignoring the noise when it gets too loud.

At the end of the day, it's not about how many stocks you chased; it's about how many smart decisions you made.

THE BOTTOM LINE

Investing isn't about chasing every rally, tip, or hot stock that your cousin's friend's uncle recommends. It's about sticking to your plan, tuning out the noise, and most importantly, avoiding impulsive decisions fuelled by FOMO. The best investors don't jump in just because "everyone else is doing it"; they wait for the right opportunities that align with their strategy. Remember, FOMO is loud, but patience should be as silent as the "P" in pool. Okay, I'll stop with the stinky jokes.

There will always be stocks on the market that shoot up 5x, 10x, or even 50x. And yes, some of them will be the ones you didn't buy. But the reality is that you're always going to miss some opportunities no matter what. It's impossible to catch every rally and trying to do so will only lead to hasty investments, panic selling, and constant regret. Instead, embrace JOMO.

☑ Rejoice because you didn't buy the hyped stocks that later crashed.
☑ Be at peace with not being in the market all the time.
☑ Invest logically, not emotionally, because discipline wins in the long run.

You won't build wealth by chasing every "hot tip", but through conviction, patience, and smart decisions. Next time someone reminds you of a stock you *"should have bought"*, just smile, sip your *chai,* and say *"Chal koi na, next time";* JOMO Zindabad!

Do not dwell in the past, do not dream of the future, concentrate the mind on the present moment.

- Buddha

19

JACK OF ALL TRADES

Would you rather try to control the rain or just take an umbrella and move forward?

Recently, I attended a big, fat wedding in Delhi, a wedding where nothing was ordinary and everything was *extravagant.* There was everything. A live Bollywood band, a pasta station dishing out fresh, cheesy treats, and dancers to ensure there was never a dull moment. Kids ran around, nosy aunties exchanged gossip faster than stock tips and the buffet was a culinary rollercoaster with offerings ranging from Manchurian to *"Tandoori sushi"*. Yes, someone decided that sushi wasn't Indian enough and gave it a tandoori twist (while I was still preparing to protest against *"Tandoori Momos").*

Amidst all this chaos, one person stood out — *Event Planner!* She seemed to be everywhere, overseeing chefs, decorators, waiters, guests, and even the occasional intoxicated uncle, all with the grace of a Bollywood heroine managing a love triangle. Watching her juggle multiple responsibilities, without breaking a sweat reminded me of Priyanka Chopra in the *What's Your Raashee?* Movie where she played twelve different roles in one movie! It was truly mesmerizing.

How did she manage all this? By remaining calm, patient, and above all, rational. She knew what needed immediate action and what could wait. She didn't panic at every little hiccup; she adapted, prioritized, and ensured the show ran smoothly.

This experience reminded me of driving on Indian roads, where you instinctively have to do a hundred things at once. You control your speed, dodge potholes the size of craters, keep an eye out for bikers who treat traffic rules as mere suggestions, and pray that no pedestrian suddenly decides to test their ninja warrior skills by jumping in front of your car. But do you stop every two seconds to consult a checklist? No, you behave rationally and navigate as required.

MARKET LENS

The stock market is a complex, constantly moving monster. Like an event planner juggling multiple responsibilities, or a driver battling through unpredictable traffic, investors have to deal with many moving parts while keeping a cool head.

This is exactly how intelligent investing works. You're constantly surrounded by moving parts, unpredictable elements, and potential distractions. But those who succeed aren't the ones who panic over every little thing; they're the ones who can weigh everything rationally and know when to act and when to maintain the course.

There is no magic formula for success in investing. However, if you want to survive and thrive in this dynamic landscape, you need to be a jack of all trades. That means being informed about company, industry, market, and global factors, including:

- **Company-specific factors:** Stock price, volume, earnings announcements, sales growth, profit margins, valuations, leverage[44], dividends, buybacks[45], acquisitions, corporate governance, etc.
- **Industry factors:** Product supply and demand, competition, market share, disruptive innovations, cyclical trends, etc.
- **Market sentiment & behaviour:** Analyst ratings, stock momentum, investor psychology, speculative activity, etc.
- **Economic indicators, and policy:** GDP[46] growth, inflation[47], interest rates[48], fiscal[49], and monetary policy[50], etc.
- **Geopolitical factors:** Trade policy, political stability, currency fluctuations, world events, etc.

---

[44] Leverage is defined as the use of borrowed funds to amplify potential returns. While leverage can increase gains, it also magnifies losses if investments go wrong.

[45] Stock Buyback or share repurchase is when a company buys back its own shares from the marketplace. This reduces the number of shares outstanding, which can increase the value of remaining shares. A buyback often signals the company believes its stock is undervalued or has excess cash.

[46] Gross Domestic Product (GDP) refers to total monetary value of all goods and services produced within a country's borders in a specific period. GDP growth is a primary indicator of a country's economic health.

[47] Inflation rate is the rate at which the general level of prices for goods and services is rising, which effectively reduces purchasing power over time. Moderate inflation is normal in a growing economy, but high inflation can erode savings and destabilize an economy.

[48] Interest rate is the cost of borrowing money or the return for lending money, usually expressed as an annual percentage. In economics, "interest rates" often refer to central bank or market rates, which influence borrowing costs, consumer spending, and investment.

[49] Fiscal policy is government decisions on taxation and spending to influence the economy. For example, cutting taxes or increasing public spending can stimulate growth (expansionary fiscal policy), while doing the opposite can slow inflation or cool an overheating economy.

[50] Monetary policy is central bank actions that manage the money supply and interest rates to control inflation and stabilize the currency. For example, a central bank may raise interest rates to cool down inflation or cut rates to stimulate borrowing and investment.

- **Consumer & social trends:** Demographic changes, consumer confidence, loyalty, changing lifestyles, etc.
- **Environmental, social, and governance (ESG) factors:** Carbon emissions, compliance with sustainability regulations, employee sentiment, working conditions, trade unions, etc.
- **Other external forces:** Supply chain disruptions, regulatory changes, commodity cycles, etc.

Feeling overwhelmed? You don't have to be. Just as a driver doesn't consciously analyze everything before making a turn, investors don't need to monitor every factor with equal intensity. With a rational mindset and a clear strategy, you can manage all these factors, filter out the noise, and focus on what's really important. Assess what's happening in the market and ask yourself, *"How does this affect my investments? What is the right decision?"*

In this chaos, keeping a cool head is your biggest advantage. And that's exactly where the **C.A.L.M.** framework comes in. It's a simple way to cut through the noise, think clearly, and invest wisely. Let me walk you through **C.A.L.M** framework:

C – Control your emotions. The biggest investing mistakes happen when fear, greed, or panic override logic. Before making a move, stop and ask yourself, *"Am I acting on logic or emotion?"*

A – Assess the big picture. Short-term market swings are just noise. What truly matters is the long-term performance of companies, industries, and economic cycles. Ask yourself, *"Does this fundamentally change my investment thesis?"*

L – Learn continuously. The best investors, like Warren Buffett and Charlie Munger, never stopped learning and neither should you. Ask yourself, *"Are you continuously upgrading your knowledge to stay ahead?"*

M – Make rational moves. Investing isn't about frequent trades; it's about smart ones. Ignore the hype, stay true to your strategy, and base decisions on research and logic. Ask yourself, *"Is your strategy aligned with your long-term goals?"*

By keeping C.A.L.M., you can train yourself to think independently, avoid emotional traps, and concentrate on what is really important. Because, in the stock market, as in life, the winner is always the one who remains calm amidst the chaos.

Did You Know ?

Investors who trade less frequently earn 6.5% more per year than those who trade impulsively. Logical investing is not about doing more; it's about doing what matters.

51

[51] Information is sourced from article published on tradecity.com titled *"24 statistics why most traders lose money"*

FROM MY JOURNEY

In my early days of investing, I took pride in having a well-diversified portfolio. A mix of IT stocks influenced by U.S. policy decisions, auto stocks affected by economic cycles, FMCG stocks responsive to inflation, and cyclical companies dependent on global demand. On paper, this strategy looked perfect However, in reality, I had unintentionally turned investing into a full-time job.

Every morning brought something new that demanded my attention. An interest rate hike by the Fed? My IT stocks would fall. A rise in fuel prices? My auto stocks would plummet. Fears of inflation? My FMCG stocks looked shaky. I tracked global indices, commodity price charts, and expert forecasts; I convinced myself that I had to react to every development

Initially, I thought this was just part of being a "serious investor", but soon I realized the truth; it wasn't about investing, it was about micro-managing the chaos. The more I tried to track and control everything, the more overwhelmed, I felt.

Then it became clear to me. The stock market will always be complex. Analyzing every detail in a rigid, theoretical way is not only impossible but also unnecessary. The real solution is to take a rational, logical approach that naturally filters out the noise.

So, I shifted my focus. Instead of becoming agitated by every short-term event, I began asking myself a simple question, *"Does this change anything about my investment thesis?"* If my IT stock has solid earnings and a growing market, why would I panic about the Fed's statements? If my FMCG stock has strong pricing power and demand, why should I follow the inflation numbers every week?

That was the moment I really understood the power of logical investing. The stock market is like a buffet with infinite possibilities. You don't have to eat everything; just choose what is really important. The moment I stopped reacting to every little thing and started thinking rationally, investing became much less stressful and far more rewarding.

That night, I opened *My Investment Diary* and wrote this down, not just as a lesson, but as a new way of thinking. Here is the relevant excerpt:

My Investment Diary

Today, I realized that closely following every detail of the markets doesn't make me a better investor, staying rational does. Now, I concentrate on what really matters. Instead of reacting to every event, I ask myself, "Does this change my investment thesis?" If it doesn't, it's just noise and will eventually correct itself if I stay rational.

Debit: "A lesson in staying rational and tuning out the market noise"
Credit: "Saved time, energy, and capital by avoiding over-analysis and unnecessary stress"
(Net balance: A sharper investor who knows that true clarity comes from focus and logical thinking)

22 Mar 2017
(Wednesday)

THE BOTTOM LINE

The stock market is a dynamic and constantly evolving landscape. As it becomes more complex, investors often feel compelled to track everything, react to everything, and control everything. But this is an illusion. The key is not to react, but to observe, reflect, and only react when necessary.

There is a famous doctrine in auditing: *"An auditor is a watchdog, not a bloodhound"*. Coined by a British judge, this principle emphasizes that an auditor must be vigilant and observant but doesn't need to chase every small discrepancy like a detective. The role is to evaluate and intervene only when necessary.

The same principle applies to investing. You don't need to react to every market fluctuation or track down every minor trend. What you need is a rational approach. Watch the market closely, but don't get carried away by emotional reactions to every little movement.

Instead of getting upset about every market change, take a step back and ask yourself, *"Does this really affect my investment thesis?"* If not, let it go. If it does, then respond logically rather than impulsively.

Much like an event planner at a wedding or a driver navigating through traffic, being a "Jack of All Trades" doesn't mean following or ignoring everything. It means knowing what is important, what is not and what is just noise, and above all, it requires always being rational and careful.

Nothing in life is to be feared, it is only to be understood.

- Marie Curie
(Polish-French physicist)

20

GO GLOBAL, GROW GLOBAL

Has something that once felt 'foreign' slowly become a part of your everyday life?

When I first moved to Delhi in 2011 for my CA studies, I thought I had a good understanding of Indian street food. Coming from Punjab, I was familiar with *samosas, pakoras,* and *chhole bhuture*. But then I saw something unfamiliar... *momos.* That was something I had rarely seen back home. Back then, *momos* in Punjab were about as common as an auto driver in Delhi agreeing to drive by the meter on the first try; technically possible, but practically impossible to find.

So, imagine my surprise when I landed in Delhi and found momo stalls on nearly every street corner. It was as if the city had undergone a silent revolution and no one had bothered to inform the rest of us. I looked at my Delhiite friend and asked, *"Bhai, har jagah momos kaise aa gaye?"* (Bro, how did momos end up everywhere?). He laughed and replied, *"Momos are the new pakoras!"*

This wasn't just a food trend; it was globalization at work. Think about it. Twenty years ago, if someone had served pizza or pasta at a Punjabi wedding, they might have been banned from the family group. Today, these dishes are practically a requirement. Oats, once considered a foreign health food, now sits alongside *parathas, poha,* and *upma* in every Indian kitchen. And let's not forget Punjab's newest addition — *Pizza Langars!* Yes, you read that right. If you thought langar meant dal, roti, and kheer, think again. Langars now also serve *Paneer Tikka Pizza!* Honestly, I wasn't sure whether to be impressed or confused.

MARKET LENS

The merging of global and local influences is not limited to food; it is also evident in what we wear, how we work, the technologies we use, and above all, where we invest. Just as our taste buds have evolved beyond *Aloo Parathas,* our investment strategies must also extend beyond local markets. The world is interconnected and thinking exclusively in terms of national boundaries is outdated. If momos are taking over Delhi and pizza is making its way into the langars of Punjab, why shouldn't global investments have a place in your portfolio?

As our tastes evolve, so should our investment approach. The stock market is no longer a single platter; it is an international buffet, offering diverse opportunities across different economies, sectors, and industries.

India is undoubtedly one of the strongest growth stories in the world today. A young population, rapid digitization, and continuous economic reforms make the next 30 years look incredibly promising. However, even the best markets experience fluctuations. Stock markets are never in a perfect equilibrium; they are either overvalued or undervalued at any given time. Relying only on a country's stock market is like eating only one dish at the buffet, even if it is overpriced.

This is where global investing comes into play. If the Indian market becomes expensive or the risk-reward ratio seems unfavourable, global investing offers a broader playing field. It allows you to diversify, manage risk better, and take advantage of growth opportunities that may not be available locally. Let's be honest: Why struggle for seats on an overcrowded local train when you can board a global flight for the same price?

Now you may be thinking, *"Can we invest in foreign markets at all?"* The answer is yes; Indian investors can invest directly in foreign stocks, although this is not yet the most common method. While direct investment in US or European stocks is legally allowed, it can be challenging due to complex account openings, higher costs, and currency conversion risks. As a result, most Indian investors prefer a simpler route and invest through global ETFs (exchange-traded funds) and mutual funds. These can be considered as "international stock platters", which is a carefully selected range of foreign companies pooled into a single fund.

Global investing is not just about long-term diversification; it also involves seizing tactical opportunities. Tactical opportunities are short-term opportunities driven by market trends, economic events, or sector-specific tailwinds. These opportunities may not last long, but if timed well, they can deliver meaningful returns. It could be a commodity surge in Australia, an upswing in US tech stocks, or a slump in interest rates across European countries. Indian investors who focus only on local markets may completely miss these windows.

Did You Know ?

In 2024, Pakistan's KSE-100 index rose nearly 60%, outperforming NIFTY and other global indices, proving that tactical global opportunities can unlock high return potential when local markets face challenges.

Suppose the Indian market is booming and all stocks seem overvalued. Instead of sitting on the sidelines, you could invest in global ETFs or mutual funds that focus on the US tech sector, Chinese manufacturing, or European industrial giants. By doing this, your portfolio will not be dependent on the market cycle of a single country. No matter what's happening locally, there's always an investment story unfolding somewhere in the world; you just need to grab your global plate and get started.

FROM MY JOURNEY

I have personally explored the global investment buffet and it has been a rewarding experience. One of my best investment decisions was to invest in U.S. technology stocks through the Edelweiss US Technology Equity Fund and the Motilal Oswal NASDAQ 100 ETF. Why did I choose these investments? When you hear names like NVIDIA, Tesla, Qualcomm, and ASML, you don't just think about companies; you think about the future. These giants are leading the way in AI, semiconductors, electric vehicles, and data processing, which are shaping the next wave of innovation. Investing in these companies through ETFs and mutual funds while sitting in India has allowed me to be part of this growth story, without needing a U.S. brokerage account or a visa interview at the U.S. embassy.

To this day, I'm still invested in those funds. The returns have been as satisfying as finding extra cheese in a pizza crust, assuming you're a fan of cheese burst. These tech innovators continue to set new benchmarks and exposure to them has not only strengthened my portfolio, but also served as a hedge against the risks in the Indian market.

However, global investments are not always about the long term. As explained earlier, they can also be a tactical move that involves recognizing short-term trends and taking advantage of them. While analysing the market data in March 2024, I noticed something interesting. NIFTY climbed to 22,500 and delivered almost 200% returns since its COVID lows. Meanwhile, China's Hang Seng Index fell to a 5-year low while most global markets reached record highs.

I know what you're thinking. China? With all its geopolitical and economic problems? Exactly! That's what makes it so interesting. The Hang Seng hadn't fallen due to fundamental weakness (or because karma was still collecting interest for one man's decision to turn a bat into brunch); it was oversold due to panic. I saw an opportunity and decided to invest in a Hang Seng ETF in March 2024.

Fast forward to October 2024. While NIFTY was up over 12%, Hang Seng ETF was up over 35%! This trade significantly outperformed the Indian markets. I took my profits, did a little victory dance (in spirit, of course), and reallocated my funds.

Performance of HANG SENG vs NIFTY

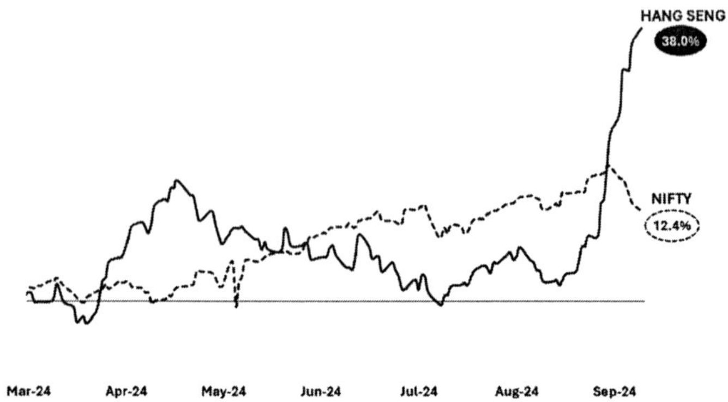

That night, I opened my diary and wrote down this lesson, because global investing is not just about diversification; it's also about seizing new opportunities beyond our country. Here's an excerpt from *My Investment Diary:*

My Investment Diary

Today, I learned first-hand why cross-border thinking can open up better investment opportunities. While the Indian market was overheated, hidden gems were available in the global markets. My decision to invest in a Hang Seng ETF instead of chasing overpriced stocks in India paid off. I learned that better opportunities can arise in other markets when a market is overvalued.

Debit: "A lesson on the importance of diversifying beyond national borders"
Credit: "Gains from trading the Hang Seng ETF, while the Indian market underperformed"
(Net balance: A smart investor who understands that growth opportunities extend far beyond domestic markets)

15 Oct 2024
(Tuesday)

THE BOTTOM LINE

Our world is shrinking, not in size, but in how effortlessly ideas, cultures, and investments cross borders. As Marshall McLuhan said in the 1960s, we now live in a *"global village"* where opportunities are no longer limited by geographical borders. Or, to put it more desi, when Honey Singh (Yo! Yo!) released the album *"International Villager"*, maybe, just maybe, he was secretly alluding to global investing. Okay, a bad joke, but you get the idea!

The stock market has gone global and so should your investment strategy. Gone are the days when you only had to focus on the domestic market when investing. Just as *momos* have found a permanent place alongside *pakoras* in Delhi, global investments should also find a place in your portfolio. India's growth story is strong, but markets go through cycles. When valuations are stretched or risks increase, international exposure can save the day.

So, the next time you review your portfolio, think beyond your home country. Whether it's through global ETFs, international mutual funds, or tactical short-term trades, there's a world of opportunity waiting for you. Investing beyond borders is about futureproofing your portfolio.

Invest wisely, explore the global buffet, and don't pile all your eggs (or potatoes, for our vegetarian friends) into one basket. The world is your oyster; think global, grow global, and let your investments reflect the limitless opportunities out there!

I am not an Athenian or a Greek, but a citizen of the world.

- Socrates
(Greek Philosopher)

21

THE NEXT BIG BET

Would you rather hold on just to prove yourself right, or let go and open yourself up to new possibilities?

They say the CFA exams are brutal and they're not wrong. But nothing truly prepares you for Level 3. It isn't just a test. It is an endurance sport disguised as a finance exam. Unlike Levels 1 and 2, which are more focused on knowledge, Level 3 tests how clearly you can think when the clock and your anxiety are racing side by side.

A close friend of mine, Vivek, had taken the exam a year earlier and shared his horror story. He knew most of the answers but managed to complete only 50 percent of the paper due to poor time management.

Unlike the objective format of the previous levels (levels 1 and 2), Level 3 features essay questions. And with these essays, you can't just muddle through; you have to be precise, quick, and strategic.

During my mock exams, I quickly realized that my old approach wasn't working — exactly as Vivek had warned. I found myself getting stuck on certain questions, explaining my answers in too much detail, and wasting valuable time.

Every time I faced a half-finished question, my mind would scream, *"Just one more sentence and it'll be perfect!"* But in doing so, I wasted the chance to even look at the other questions.

Frustrated, I turned to my teacher, an experienced CFA professional. He listened patiently as I rambled on about my strategy, then stopped me with a simple but powerful question:

"Do you want to pass the exam, or do you want to complete every question?"

This one sentence struck me like a lightning bolt. I had been so focused on achieving perfection that I sabotaged my own success. My obsession with fully answering every question prevented me from completing the exam. So, I did something that went against my instincts. I let go of my old habits and forced myself to move on when the time was up, even if I hadn't finished my answer.

Fast forward to today:

- ✦ *Did I answer every question perfectly?* ***No.***
- ✦ *Did I stick to my time management strategy?* ***Yes.***
- ✦ *Did I pass the CFA?* ***Absolutely Yes.***

This experience taught me a life-changing lesson. Sometimes, you need to let go of outdated methods and adopt new strategies to succeed. And that, my friend, is exactly what successful investors do. If you think this lesson applies only to exams, just wait until you see how it plays out in the stock market.

MARKET LENS

Let me ask you a question: *"Do you want to make money, or do you just want to make money from a particular stock?"*

Sounds like a no-brainer, doesn't it? Yet, time and again, investors become so attached to certain stocks that they refuse to let them go, even when it's clear that holding on is causing more harm than good.

Take Kodak, for example. Once a giant in the photography industry, Kodak was as synonymous with cameras as Xerox is with photocopies (yes, Xerox is the name of the brand that sells printers). At its peak, the company held more than 80% of the US camera market. If you wanted to capture a memory, you reached for Kodak film.

However, with the advent of the digital age, Kodak refused to accept the change and clung to its old film-based business model, convinced that its dominance was unshakeable. The result? Kodak filed for bankruptcy in 2012. The stock price plummeted, losing over 90% of its value. But many loyal investors, especially those who had once thrived through Kodak's golden age, clung to their shares, refusing to accept that the world had moved on. They indulged in nostalgia, while the stock market has little interest in such sentiments.

Did You Know ?

Kodak invented the digital camera in 1975 but refused to commercialize it, ultimately leading to its downfall, largely due to the very technology it created.

If Kodak represents the danger of clinging to the past, then Zomato serves as a great example of embracing the new frontiers.

When Zomato went public on the Indian stock exchange, its valuation exceeded the combined market capitalization of all listed hotels and restaurants in India. Traditional investors were shocked. *"How can a food delivery company be valued higher than century-old restaurant chains?"*

But here's the thing. Zomato is not a restaurant! It's a digital, scalable, technology-driven company that fits perfectly into the modern consumer lifestyle. It's not about comparing apples to oranges; it's about recognizing that the market landscape has changed.

If someone had invested only in textile mills, copper wiring, and VCR manufacturing in the 1980s, industries that were booming at the time, they would have been wiped out as technology advanced and new industries emerged. Imagine if someone had thought in the early 2000s that landlines, DVDs, and print media would be around forever. Today, they would've wondered why their portfolio looks like an archaeological exhibit. Take a look at the below:

- **1990s:** Those who bet on the rise of software and IT services (Infosys, TCS, and Wipro) turned small investments into big fortunes.
- **2000s:** Those who were early believers in telecom made a fortune as mobile connectivity exploded.
- **2010s:** The rise of e-commerce, FinTech, and digital platforms gave birth to giants like Amazon, PayPal, and Paytm.

Today, we are on the brink of another wave of transformation. The next multi-bagger stocks and disruptive industries are likely to emerge from sectors that are just starting to take off. This could be Artificial Intelligence (AI) and Machine Learning (ML), or Electric Vehicles (EV) and Clean Energy, or Blockchain and Web 3.0, or Space Technology and Satellite Communications.

The pattern is clear. Industries are changing, disruptors are emerging, and the biggest profits are made by those who invest in the future rather than the past. The key to long-term investment success lies not only in sticking to what is safe but also in investing with foresight in the winners of tomorrow.

FROM MY JOURNEY

Let me share the story of my friend and his infamous Yes Bank saga, a perfect example of how holding on to the past can cloud sound judgment.

At its peak, Yes Bank was the poster child of India's banking revolution. It was loved by analysts, favoured among retail investors, and a stock that seemed destined for growth. At its peak, the stock price soared to ₹380 and everyone was singing as loudly as the contestants on Indian Idol. My friend was a die-hard fan of Yes Bank, convinced that this stock was his ticket to financial glory.

Then reality struck. Reports of financial irregularities emerged and the stock began to decline. It fell to ₹180.

While many investors recognised the warning signs, my friend viewed this as a unique buying opportunity. *"Aur kitna hi girega?"* (Come on, how much more can it fall?) he said confidently and doubled his investment. His logic? *"Yes Bank is a solid institution and it's only a matter of time before it recovers!"*

Spoiler alert: It didn't recover. Instead of bouncing back, it crashed. The stock price crashed to ₹40. My friend, however, was not discouraged. Instead of cutting his losses, he bought even more, convinced that this had to be the bottom. By then, Yes Bank made up almost 60% of his portfolio, with an average purchase price of ₹200. Every time the stock fell, he would say to himself, *"Bas, ab aur kitna hi girega"*. He said, *"I'll wait until I can sell it at my purchase price: no profit, no loss"*.

Then came the final blow. RBI imposed a moratorium on Yes Bank (a moratorium is something like a strategic time-out in cricket when things are going badly. RBI steps in, restricts deposits and withdrawals, and lets the bank catch its breath to avoid a total collapse). The stock price didn't just fall; it nosedived into single digits, wiping out fortunes and turning optimism into sheer panic.

Even then, he refused to sell. That was over four years ago now. Yes Bank is a shadow of its former self. While my friend clung to his emotional attachment, he missed out on countless other investment opportunities. The real loss was not just the fall in the stock price, but the opportunity cost of not investing the money elsewhere. Here is a snapshot of Yes Bank's stock price, capturing the entire saga through numbers:

"Yes Bank" Stock Price Chart

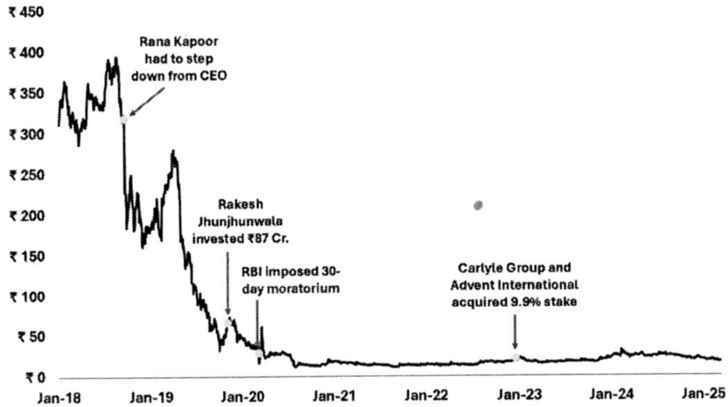

The Yes Bank saga reminds me of what I call the *"Devasena Syndrome"*. Just like *Devasena* in *Baahubali*, who waited for years hoping her son would come back and rescue her, some investors keep holding on, waiting for a miracle turnaround. In the movie, it works; Mahendra Baahubali comes back and restores the throne. However, in the stock market, *"Darling Prabhas"* is not coming. Lost stocks don't always make a heroic comeback. More often than not, waiting for a fallen stock to magically return to its former glory only leads to disappointment, not redemption.

A stock doesn't owe you a comeback just because you once believed in it. Never let emotions guide your investment decisions. It's okay to move on because holding onto a stock for too long can cost you more than just money. In the stock market, hope is not a strategy.

Reflecting on my friend's mistake that night, I realized that his loss was a valuable lesson for me. So, I opened *My Investment Diary* and wrote it down:

My Investment Diary

Today, I learned that investing is about looking forward, not clinging to the past. Holding on to a failed stock out of attachment can be costly, not only in terms of losses but also in terms of missed opportunities to invest in the future.

When the fundamentals change, it is wiser to move on and focus on future possibilities, rather than waiting for a past winner to make a comeback.

Debit: "A lesson in focusing on future potential rather than clinging to the past"
Credit: "Capital secured by avoiding the Yes Bank debacle"
(Net balance: A smart investor who adapts, evolves, and makes decisions with a forward-looking mindset)

05 Mar 2020
(Thursday)

THE BOTTOM LINE

Embrace new realities, let go of what no longer works, and look for fresh opportunities. Holding on to the past, whether it's an outdated strategy or a failing stock, only leads to greater losses. The stock market doesn't care about emotional attachment, just like it didn't care about Kodak's legacy or Yes Bank's former glory.

The biggest mistake isn't picking the wrong stocks but refusing to move forward. Just as I had to adapt for my CFA exam, investors must evolve with changing market dynamics. The world won't wait. Ask yourself, *"Do you invest in yesterday's winners or tomorrow's market leaders?"*

The secret of change is to focus all your energy not on fighting the old, but on building the new.

- Socrates
(Greek Philosopher)

GOOD DEBT, BAD DEBT

Have you ever wondered why big companies take out loans even when they have plenty of money? What do they know that you don't?

There is a popular book by Robert Kiyosaki called *Rich Dad Poor Dad.* If you haven't read it, you might assume it's like the financial equivalent of *Kabhi Khushi Kabhi Gham,* where Shah Rukh Khan grows up rich only to discover that his real financial father is not Amitabh Bachchan, but someone who's struggling to make ends meet. However, that's not the case.

If Kiyosaki had the narrative flair of Karan Johar, there might be dramatic violin music, an indebted father wiping his tears, and a business-savvy uncle swooping in to save the day, probably dressed in a designer sherwani. Fortunately, Kiyosaki skips the melodrama and gets straight to the point. His book isn't about DNA test results and family reunions; it's about two completely different approaches to money, which he views through the lens of his two father figures:

- **Poor Dad (his own father):** A man who believed in saving every rupee, avoiding debt like a pothole on an Indian road, and playing it safe.
- **Rich Dad (his best friend's father):** An entrepreneur who viewed debt as a tool, took calculated risks, and believed that money worked for him.

The biggest twist in the story? Not all debts are bad. To "Poor Dad", debt was like an unwanted relative who only shows up when he needs money — stressful and best avoided. On the other hand, "Rich Dad" saw debt as a tool that, when used wisely, could build wealth rather than destroy it. So, debt itself isn't the problem; understanding its purpose is crucial. Let's take a look at that.

☑ Taking a loan to buy an 85-inch TV just to watch the IPL in 4K quality? That's bad debt. Sure, Virat Kohli will look fantastic, but EMI[52] will haunt you long after the season is over.

☒ Taking out a loan to invest in a business, stocks, or rental properties? That's good debt. Instead of depleting your finances every month, this kind of debt helps you bring money back into your pocket.

There are two types of debt. One works for you like a smart employee, while the other works against you like a lazy intern who keeps missing deadlines. Most of us grew up hearing the phrase, *"Debt is bad. Avoid loans. Pay cash"*. But the truth is, debt itself is neither good nor bad; it's how you use it that

[52] Equated Monthly Installment (EMI) is A fixed monthly payment made by a borrower to repay both interest and principal on a loan. Common in home and auto loans.

matters. In this chapter, I aim to change your perspective on debt. By the end, you will no longer see debt as a burden but as a tool that, if used correctly, can lead you to new financial heights.

MARKET LENS

Big companies understand debt differently than most individuals do. Instead of fearing it, they leverage borrowed money to amplify their returns. They borrow at low interest rates to fund high-growth investments, expanding businesses, acquiring assets, and building long-term wealth.

Take Reliance Industries, for example. Mukesh Ambani strategically took on debt to expand business. Did he take loans to buy luxury yachts? No. He used that debt to build *Jio,* disrupt an entire industry, and create billions in wealth. Similarly, real estate developers don't use their own money to buy land; they take out loans, develop the property, sell it for a profit, and then pay back the loan while reaping returns.

Now, let's bring this concept to the stock market. Investors have a powerful tool at their disposal: *Margin Trading Funding (MTF)*[53]. With MTF, you pledge your existing stocks as collateral to borrow money from your broker, allowing you to buy more shares than your own capital would permit. This strategy enables you to amplify potential gains, but it also comes with risks because just as profits can multiply, so can losses.

---

[53] Margin trading funding refers to using borrowed money from a broker to buy more stocks than one could with just their own cash. The investor's existing holdings serve as collateral. While margin (leverage) can amplify gains if the stock rises, it also magnifies losses and can lead to debt if the trade goes wrong.

Think of it like using a credit card to invest in stocks. If the stock price rises, your returns grow exponentially. But if the price falls, the losses can accumulate just as fast. That's why successful investors treat leveraged debt with precision, like a scalpel, not a hammer.

The distinction between good debt and bad debt is crucial in investing. Taking out a loan for an 85-inch TV is bad debt because it drains your wealth without generating returns. On the other hand, using debt strategically through MTF or other leveraged investments can be good debt, but only if managed wisely.

Debt isn't the enemy. It's how you use it that matters. If you understand its potential, debt can become a powerful ally in wealth creation, both in business and the stock market.

Myth Vs Reality

Myth: Paying off a loan early is always the smartest financial move.
Reality: If your loan costs 7–8% but you can invest at 12–15%, keeping the loan and investing the surplus could be beneficial.

FROM MY JOURNEY

I was never fond of debt. In fact, I strictly refused to borrow money, whether it was loans, credit cards, or the so-called "easy EMI" traps. My philosophy was simple. If I couldn't pay for it in cash, I didn't buy it. I preferred to save for months, even years, rather than owe someone a single rupee. Whether it was the latest gadget, a dream vacation, or a car nothing, not even for a legitimate purpose like a business or an investment was worth going into debt for. It was a clear no for me, much like a strict hostel warden refusing late-night entry — *no excuses, no negotiations.* So, when the debt came knocking on my door, I pretended I wasn't home.

In hindsight, I realize I wasn't just avoiding debt; I was a true *debt atheist.* The idea that debt could be anything other than a burden seemed absurd to me. I viewed it as a financial sin that only led to stress, financial instability, and sleepless nights.

At the time, I believed I was acting sensibly and making the right decisions. However, as I gained more experience in investing, I began to question my rigid beliefs. If big companies borrow to expand, why should individuals refrain from doing so? If billionaires were borrowing to increase their wealth, was I simply playing it too safe? Could debt actually be a tool, rather than a trap?

Over time, I have questioned my mindset and accepted the idea of *good debt,* borrowing money for productive purposes such as investment, education, or starting a business. But one thing hasn't changed: I'm still firmly against borrowing for leisure and lifestyle improvements. Taking debt for depreciating assets like the latest gadget, an extravagant vacation, or a swanky car? Still a definite no for me.

I have transitioned from being a *"debt atheist"* to a *"bad debt atheist".* While I no longer oppose all forms of debt, I remain steadfast about borrowing for things that have no long-term benefit. It's not just about avoiding debt; it's about knowing which debt is worth taking on and which debt is just a financial trap in disguise. My curiosity led me to test this belief.

Here's what I did. In 2021, I took out a personal loan, but instead of buying a car or financing a vacation, I invested it in quality stocks. Sounds reckless? That may be. But I had a plan. Instead of letting the debt crush me, I made it work for me:

1. I pledged the stocks I bought to generate margin.
2. I used this margin to sell options (which I have explained in detail in the next chapter titled "Double Ka Meetha Strategy").
3. The additional income from selling options covered my interest on the loan, while my stocks continued to rise in value.

It felt like a perfect balancing act; the investment was growing, the loan was paying for itself, and I wasn't stuck in an endless EMI cycle with nothing to show for it. Over time, this strategy has significantly increased my wealth. Here's an excerpt from *My Investment Diary:*

My Investment Diary

Today, I have realized that the problem is not debt, but the misuse of debt. If used wisely, it can be a powerful tool for growth. My decision to take out a loan and invest strategically has shown me that debt, when planned correctly, can work for me and not against me.

The key is to use debt to build assets. If they help me grow financially, they are an advantage, not a burden.

Debit: "A lesson on the wise use of debt as a means of wealth creation"
Credit: "Higher returns through the strategic integration of debt into my investment approach"
(Net balance: A smart investor who knows that good debt, if used wisely, can be a catalyst for financial growth)

20 Aug 2024
(Tuesday)

Instead of fearing debt, I have learned to control and optimize it. To be clear, this is not a "get-rich-quick" hack. There are risks involved and it's not for everyone. At this point, the old WWE disclaimer comes to mind, *"These stunts are performed by professionals. Don't try this at home!"* My advice? It's best to get advice from a professional before you get involved. Here's what I've realized:

✦ Debt is like fire. It can cook your food or burn down your house; it all depends on how you use it.

✦ A well-thought-out debt strategy can accelerate wealth building rather than hold you back.

- Being debt-free isn't always the goal; being financially smart is.

The biggest change for me was not only in my portfolio but also in my mindset. I no longer saw debt as a burden; I began to view it as a tool that, if used wisely, can promote financial growth.

THE BOTTOM LINE

Debt isn't always the bad guy; it's how you use it that matters. Bad debt is like the friend who always borrows money, but never pays you back; it empties your wallet and limits your financial growth. Good debt, on the other hand, is like a reliable business partner that helps you grow your wealth. It works for you, not against you. The trick is not to fear debt but to understand it.

Think about it, even the biggest companies in the world take on massive debt. Is that because they are broke? No. It's because they know how to use low-interest debt to generate higher returns. They borrow wisely, invest smartly, and create more wealth for their shareholders.

The next time you're considering taking out a loan, ask yourself, *"Will this debt create an asset or just increase my liabilities?"* Or will it put money in my pocket or take money out of it?

If it works for you, it's a good debt. When it works against you, you know what to do. Smart debt isn't a burden; it's a tool. And like any tool, it can help you shape your financial future if you use it right.

What we call common sense is often nothing more than a collection of prejudices.

- Albert Einstein
(German theoretical physicist)

23

"DOUBLE KA MEETHA" STRATEGY

Do you feel great when life offers a little unexpected delight, like a surprise upgrade or a bonus you didn't see coming?

If you've ever been to Hyderabad, you've probably heard of *Double ka Meetha.* This rich dessert, similar to *Shahi Tukda,* which is popular in parts of North India. It consists of deep-fried bread drenched in sugar syrup and topped with a creamy layer of *Rabri.* But have you ever wondered why it's called *Double ka Meetha?*

The name originates from the old custom of calling the bread "double roti" because it puffs up to twice its size when baked, although I honestly think it was just meant to sound fancy. But I have my own theory called *Double ka Meetha* because it's twice as sweet, first from the syrup-drenched bread and then from the rich *Rabri* on top. Think of it as a dessert that surprises you with an extra dose of joy. And if there's one thing I love, whether it's eating or investing; it's getting more than what I signed up for!

When you take a bite, the first hit of sugar comes from the syrupy bread. Just when you think that's it, the *Rabri* comes along and elevates the experience to a whole new level. That's what makes *Double ka Meetha* so special, it fills you up while also doubling the satisfaction. Similarly, I have an investment strategy that follows the same philosophy, which I call the *Double ka Meetha* strategy a.k.a. DKM strategy.

Most investors believe that returns can only be achieved through price increases. But what if I told you there's a way to add a second layer of returns to your portfolio, like a surprising amount of *Rabri?* Are you curious? Read on, because I am about to turn your portfolio into the *Double Ka Meetha* of wealth!

MARKET LENS

The first layer of sweetness in your investment journey comes from portfolio returns, you invest in stocks, they perform well, and you enjoy a nice return. This is akin to the sugar-soaked bread of *Double ka Meetha* — sweet, satisfying, and exactly what you signed up for. But if you settle for just that, it's like eating dry bread without the syrup; why settle for less when you can get that extra *Rabri* of return.

This is where DKM strategy comes into play. So, what is this magical second layer of sweetness? Here's the secret. I make my existing portfolio work overtime by pledging my stocks. Instead of sitting idle in my demat account, my stocks help me generate extra income; imagine it as renting out an extra room in your house instead of leaving it unused. When you pledge your stocks to a broker, you have access to margin limits, i.e., extra funds that you can trade without selling your stocks. It's like your portfolio is working a second shift while you sit back and enjoy the returns.

What do I do with this additional margin? I sell OOTM[54] (out of the money) options, which are options where the strike price is less favourable than the current market price, making them cheaper but lower in the probability of execution. If this phrase sounds complex, don't worry. The concept becomes simple once you grasp its logic.

Here's the gist:

- When you sell options, you collect a premium upfront, as if you're getting paid before the actual work is done.
- Over time, the likelihood of these options being exercised decreases, allowing you to keep the premium without much effort.
- This allows you to generate passive income from your portfolio.

Why is this strategy a game changer? The beauty of the DKM strategy is that it works in all market situations, whether the market is rising, falling, or simply doing nothing. With this strategy, I've managed to generate an additional 5-7% return per year on my portfolio using passive trading, i.e., with minimal effort. If you can master active trading strategies, this additional income could exceed 5-7%. The sky's not the limit; it's just the beginning.

Need more clarity? The graphics below give you a quick snapshot of how the strategy works:

---

[54] Out of the money (OOTM) options are contracts that currently have no intrinsic value because they can't currently be exercised for a profit. But they still hold value, based on their potential to turn profitable before their expiration date if the market moves in their favour.

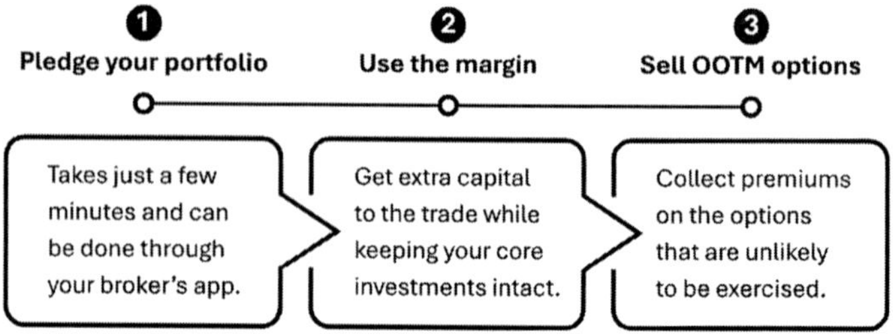

With this strategy, you can add an extra layer of returns to your existing portfolio, just as *Double ka Meetha* is not complete without the creamy *Rabri.* However, just like too much dessert can lead to a sugar crash, this strategy works best in moderation; overdoing it can be risky, so it's important to know where to stop.

Did You Know ?

Even big investors pledge their stocks. Promoters of big companies like Vedanta, Zee Entertainment, and even Reliance have pledged stocks to raise capital for business expansion.

FROM MY JOURNEY

Now I would share how I applied the DKM strategy in my own trading account. I have pledged my portfolio to generate margin limits, which I then use for trading. I'm not a full-time trader glued to a screen all day analyzing every tick and candlestick pattern. In fact, I often rely on the expertise of a close friend who is a full-time trader. And remember, *"These stunts are performed by professionals. Don't try this at home!"* i.e., always get advice from a professional before diving in.

Currently, I take it a step further by making my margin work double shifts like a workaholic who doesn't believe in office hours.

- ✦ During trading hours, I use my margin to trade equity derivatives.
- ✦ When the stock market closes at 15:30, I don't just call it a day. Instead, I reuse the same margin for the commodities market, which stays open until 23:30.
- ✦ This approach allows me to deploy my capital twice a day, effectively doubling the return on my portfolio.

Now, before you think this is a magical wealth hack, let's be honest, this is not a foolproof strategy. It comes with risks and costs such as brokerage fees, taxes, and interest can eat into profits if not managed well. But with discipline and smart execution, the returns can far outweigh the costs.

Over time, this strategy has significantly boosted my portfolio's performance, much like an extra *Rabri* on an already delicious, sweet loaf of bread. When I reviewed my portfolio at the end of the year, I made a note in *My Investment Diary.* Here's an excerpt:

My Investment Diary

Today, I learned that option strategies can be a smart way to generate additional income for an existing portfolio. By pledging my stocks and using the margin to sell options, I created a source of passive income.

It's not about taking bigger risks; it's about using the resources wisely. If you do it right, this approach brings additional returns and makes the portfolio work better.

Debit: "A lesson in increasing returns through strategic options trading"
Credit: "Additional income through effective leveraging of my portfolio"
(Net balance: A smart investor who recognized the power of option strategies in building a steady passive income)

31 Dec 2023
(Sunday)

As with dessert, moderation is necessary here itself. Too much sugar can lead to problems and excessive leverage can do the same. Start slowly, understand what you're doing and remember — *"patience is a virtue!"* If you do it right, the reward is as sweet as it gets.

THE BOTTOM LINE

Double ka Meetha isn't just a dessert; it's a clever investment strategy that can double the sweetness of your returns. By pledging your portfolio and using the margin-to-trade options, you create an extra layer of passive income in addition to your regular portfolio returns. If you're strategic and careful, this approach works in any market situation and provides an extra dose of profitability without changing your core investments.

But don't be like a Bollywood hero running through a maze of plot lines; charming, but completely clueless about where the story is going. Start slowly, be aware of the risks and never over-leverage yourself. If necessary, consult a financial advisor before you get started. The goal is to increase your returns, not gamble.

With the right execution, the DKM strategy can become your secret recipe for compounding wealth; just like the perfect blend of crusty bread, sugar syrup, and Rabri makes *Double ka Meetha* an unforgettable treat.

So, invest wisely, manage risk, and build your wealth like a perfectly balanced dessert — rich, layered, and with just the right amount of sweetness!

The difference between ordinary and extraordinary is that little extra.

- Jimmy Johnson
(American football coach)

CTRL + ALT + 'ALGO'

If your phone's contact list disappeared right now, how many numbers could you dial from memory?

People who grew up in the 90s or early 2000s had an elite superpower of memorising phone numbers. Not only did we know our own number, but we also remembered the home landline, our best friend's number, the neighbour's emergency contact, and even our school principal's number (for reasons unknown). Parents, of course, were like walking phone books, effortlessly reciting relatives' numbers faster than a train announcer at New Delhi railway station.

Then came mobile phones. At first, we simply saved numbers, but soon we stopped manually dialling them. And before we knew it, voice assistants took over, making even button presses unnecessary. Now, a simple command like *"Hey Siri, call Dad"* gets the job done instantly.

I no longer remember my wife's mobile phone number. The woman I share my life with, who I tag on Instagram with *"I need a vacation"*, and who will answer my SOS call (well, "probably will" after reading this chapter) when I'm stranded on the highway at 2 AM... yeah, I have no idea what her number is.

Nothing prepares you for the death stare when an online portal asks for her number and I have to sheepishly say, *"Um…wait, let me check"*. The judgment, the disappointment, the dramatic *"You don't even know my number?"* moment. If looks could kill, I'd be six feet under.

And yet, I still remember a random landline number: 264421. It's been sitting rent-free in my brain for two decades and I'll never get closure. Maybe it belonged to a long-lost friend. Maybe it was a wrong number that I accidentally memorized. Or maybe it was my past life's demat account helpline. I'll never know.

At some point, we simply stopped bothering. We didn't wake up one day and announce, *"From now on, I refuse to memorize numbers!"* It just… happened. No protests, no nostalgia, no farewell to the era of memorized numbers.

Because let's be honest, if a machine can do something better, why should we waste our brain cells? This trend extends beyond phone numbers. We've outsourced tasks to technology faster than a typical Indian family delegates wedding preparations to a single overworked cousin.

Take birthdays. In the past, remembering birthdays was a sign of true friendship. And today? Facebook, Google, and WhatsApp remind us, often with unnecessary fireworks and a virtual cake. If the app didn't remind you, did that birthday even happen?

Look at how we handle money. Our parents counted cash, stacked banknotes neatly, and hid emergency funds under mattresses. A trip to the bank was a half-day event that required passbooks, chequebooks, and a lot of patience. Today? UPI is king. Even the sabziwala has a QR code and if you dare say, *"Bhaiya, Cash?"*, he will roll his eyes as if you had asked for a handwritten bill at D-Mart.

Driving has changed, too. In the past, you had to ask for directions and rely on vague instructions like, *"Keep going straight. You'll spot a big tree, and there'll be a narrow lane just to its left"*. And now? We've Google Maps. We follow it blindly, even if it leads us trustingly into a lake.

The common denominator? We have never resisted these changes. We didn't debate whether UPI was "real" banking or whether Google Maps was making us lazy. We simply accepted them. So when it comes to changes in stock market trading, why should we treat them any differently?

MARKET LENS

With Google Maps, navigation became objective, offering real-time traffic updates, the fastest routes, and a polite voice that gently suggests, *"Please take a U-turn"* if you've clearly made a wrong turn.

That's exactly what algo trading is. Algo (or Algorithmic) trading is a strategy that uses computer programs to automate the process of buying and selling financial instruments based on predefined conditions. In the past, short-term trading was manual, i.e., reading charts, recognizing trends, and timing orders. Traders had to sit in front of screens, interpret candlestick patterns like astrologers decipher destiny, and manually execute buy/sell orders. Some got it right, most got burned, and all endured emotional turmoil. Then came algo trading, automating all objective trading tasks.

In India, algo trading has surged, driven by the rise of specialized firms. Data from the National Stock Exchange (NSE) reveals that algo trading accounts for over 50% of equity cash segment trades and 70% of derivatives trades. This is a staggering shift in just a few years.

In the past, this magic was only for the big boys. *Hedge funds*[55], *High-Frequency Traders*[56], and financial institutions had exclusive access to sophisticated models, executing trades within milliseconds. Retail investors? They were like cab drivers in a world rapidly switching to self-driving cars.

With user-friendly algo platforms, even small investors can automate short-term trades. You don't need expensive infrastructure or a PhD in programming. Just set your logic, define your rules, and let the system execute trades while you sip *chai.*

But there's a catch! Google Maps will get you to your destination, but it won't ask if you're heading in the right direction to begin with. Enter the wrong location, and it will efficiently guide you straight to the wrong place.

Algo trading works the same way. If your logic is flawed, your indicators are arbitrary, or your stop-loss levels make no sense, then algos will automate your failure with just as much speed and precision. It's called GIGO: *"Garbage in, garbage out (GIGO)"* and the market doesn't make exceptions. Let me summarise.

---

[55] Hedge Funds is a private investment fund that uses advanced strategies (leverage, short selling, derivatives, etc.) to seek high returns. Hedge funds are typically open only to institutional investors or high-net-worth individuals and are less regulated than mutual funds.

[56] High-frequency trading (HFT) is a form of algorithmic trading that executes numerous trades at extremely fast speeds, capitalizing on small price changes.

What Algo Trading CAN DO:

☑ **No emotions, just execution:** No more panic selling because of a red candle or FOMO buying at the peak. The algo follows logic, not mood swings.

☑ **Passive income, active returns:** Your money works for you without requiring you to stare at a screen all day.

☑ **Customizable to your risk appetite:** You control the logic. Conservative trend following? Risk-managed position trades? You decide. The algo follows orders.

☑ **Time saving:** If you're tired of staring at charts all day and reading *"Head & Shoulders"* patterns (which look like shampoo logos), this is for you.

What Algo Trading CAN NOT DO:

☒ **Not a substitute for long-term investing:** If short-term trading is like Google Maps, long-term investing is like choosing the right target. Algo trading does not replace the need for fundamental research, rational thinking, or understanding a company's long-term potential.

☒ **Not a sure money machine:** Algorithms do not guarantee profits. They only automate execution. Bad strategy = bad results. Period.

☒ **Don't "set it and forget it":** Unlike a good biryani recipe, you can't just set algo trades and expect delicious profits every time. You need to adjust, optimise, and monitor their performance.

Algo trading is not a magic formula for success, nor a guaranteed path to profits. It's a tool. Powerful when used wisely, ruthless when mismanaged. Done right, it eliminates human bias, ensures disciplined execution, and removes emotion from trading decisions. Done wrong, it can magnify losses faster than a bad crypto tip in a Telegram group.

FROM MY JOURNEY

I'll be honest, initially, I thought algo trading was just another gimmick. There are already enough new formula investment hacks, trading bots, and WhatsApp stock tips in the stock market claiming to make you rich overnight. I had already burned my hands trying to outsmart the market with manual trading. Analysing charts, chasing trends, and thinking I could time my way to riches. So, when I heard that retail investors were using algorithmic strategies, my first reaction was, *"This is probably just another modern-day scam"*.

In my mind, anything that automated trading had to be a scam; probably something dreamed up by a 21-year-old *financial guru* with a ring light and a YouTube channel. I'd seen too many flashy Instagram ads: *"Invest ₹10,000, make ₹50,000 a day!"*. A plan so good that even Ambani must be wondering why he never tried it.

But then a friend, a senior colleague whom I really respect and trust, mentioned that he had taken algo-trading as his profession. He wasn't just experimenting; he was developing Python-based algo strategies, optimising them, and using them professionally. At first, I thought, *"Good for him. But I Have Doubts"*.

Then, one day, during a conversation over coffee, he explained how it actually works. *"You don't have to do anything manually"*, he said, sipping his cappuccino as if he were describing something as normal as ordering food on Zomato:

"You simply connect your demat account to an algo platform, set the rules, and it places the trades for you. Automatically".

As someone who has traded manually for years, this was a crazy concept for me. Trades being executed on my demat account without me having to lift a finger? No more staring at the charts, no more second-guessing, no more panic selling because of a red candle?

It sounded too simple. Too suspiciously simple. So, like any good sceptic, I decided to test it. I linked my Demat account to the Algo platform (a third-party app) via an API, which in simple terms meant I gave it permission to trade on my behalf. My friend set up his strategy and that was it. No manual intervention was required.

And then the magic began. I opened my trading account and saw call/put options being traded in real time, without me having to do anything. Buy orders, sell orders, adjustments; everything happened faster than I could react. At this point, two important thoughts crossed my mind:

"This is madness. What if something goes wrong? What if I wake up tomorrow and my portfolio is emptier than an SBI bank branch at lunchtime?"

"Wait… a minute... this actually works?"

I'm not exaggerating, but the returns were unreal. It wasn't just a few small, insignificant gains; I made real, consistent profits over time. Unlike my usual trading experiences (which involved emotional breakdowns and regretting life decisions), this was stress-free.

Myth Vs Reality

Myth: Algo trading = guaranteed profits.
Reality: Algos don't predict the future; they only follow your logic. A bad strategy executed automatically is still a bad strategy.

There were no doubts, no impulsive actions, and no *"What if I sell now and the price goes up?"* Just pure logic flawlessly executed.

That was the moment when I realized that algo-trading wasn't a gimmick or a scam; it was just automation done right. The system simply followed the logic I approved, executed the trades precisely, and eliminated the biggest mistake in trading — *human emotion.*

And the best part? I didn't have to do anything. It worked while I was busy living my life. That's when I knew, I had underestimated algo trading all along. Honestly? I've never looked at trading the same way since. When I reviewed my portfolio at the end of the year, I made a note in *My Investment Diary.* Here's an excerpt:

My Investment Diary

Today, I learned that algo-trading is easier than I thought and can bring big profits. I always believed that short-term trading required constant monitoring and human decisions. However, after automating my trades, I realized that execution can be better when emotions are muted.

No more second-guessing, no more panic selling: just clear, logical execution.

Debit: "A lesson on using algo-trading to simplify execution and increase returns"
Credit: "Profits achieved through automated trading strategies"
(Net balance: A smart trader who knows that automation makes trading easier and more effective)

31 Dec 2023
(Sunday)

THE BOTTOM LINE

If something makes life easier, we accept it without hesitation. We've stopped memorizing phone numbers, we've replaced physical maps with Google Maps, and we no longer question UPI payments. So why should short-term trading be stuck in the past?

Algo trading is not magic. It's not a get-rich-quick hack. It's just logic, automated. It won't turn a bad strategy into a profitable one, but it will execute a good strategy better than you ever could.

Trading is about precision, speed, and objectivity. And humans? We are emotional. We hesitate, we overthink, we panic, we experience FOMO. The algo doesn't do that.

That's the advantage. So, if you're looking to trade short-term, why rely on human flaws when you can depend on pure execution?

Set the rules. Let the algo do the rest. Because when it comes to trading, execution wins.

We cannot solve our problems with the same thinking we used when we created them.

- Albert Einstein
(German theoretical physicist)

25

PENNY SAVED = PENNY EARNED

Have you ever held on to something for too long just because you didn't want to admit to yourself that it was time to let go?

We've all dreamed of getting fit, building a six-pack, and living a healthier, more active life. And naturally, like every fitness enthusiast, you head to the gym.

Do you remember your first day at the gym? You walked in, excited, already picturing yourself walking out as Chris Hemsworth (or John Abraham for Bollywood flair), wearing a muscle-hugging t-shirt and moving effortlessly in slow motion.

Then the gym manager, who is also the trainer, the cleaner, and sometimes even the guy who fixes the AC (small gyms are basically run by superheroes), makes you an offer you can't refuse:

"Sign up for an annual membership at half price. Save big today!"

It's a steal deal and your excitement leads you to sign up for the long-term package, convinced that this time, everything will be different.

You can already imagine yourself working out every day, sipping protein shakes like a post-workout ritual, and of course, posting gym selfies (let's face it, among all the equipment, the mirror is the most overused piece in any gym).

But then... reality sets in. Work deadlines start to pile up. Social obligations take over. Your enthusiasm fades, faster than your New Year's resolutions.

Slowly but surely, you start skipping workouts. At first, it's just once or twice, and you tell yourself, *"I'll go tomorrow"*. Then weeks pass and before you know it, your gym fees become a silent observer on your bank statement, deducted monthly while you sit on the couch eating potato chips (*alright,* sweet potato chips). A few months later, you finally accept the truth. You've barely used your membership. What once felt like a steal deal now feels like money down the drain.

At that point, most people feel stuck, frustrated by the sunk cost and unsure what to do next. But here's the thing: even if you haven't used it much, all is not lost.

Many gyms allow you to freeze your membership for a small fee. It's like hitting the pause button on your fitness journey until your life settles down. Or, if you're clever, you could sell the remaining months of your membership to a friend who still believes in the gym dream (there's always one who hasn't caught the *"I'm too busy"* bug).

Either way, whether you pause it or sell it, you're salvaging some value from your gym fees. What if I told you that you can follow the same principle in the investing world? What if protecting your profits is just as important as earning new ones?

MARKET LENS

Let's shift to the stock market. Imagine you bought a stock after a market dip. The stock doubled in value within a few months, thanks to a *bull market*[57] rally. Now you're sitting on 100% returns. Sounds like a dream, right?

But here's the twist. You haven't booked profits yet. There are two ways this story can go:

1) Holding on without booking profits
   You hold on, waiting for more. Then the market turns. The bull run fades, and *bear market*[58] take over. Within weeks, the stock falls sharply. Often, the ones that rise the fastest also fall the hardest. Your gains vanish. You're back to your original buying price. You've made zero return, despite seeing your portfolio in green.

2) Booking partial profits
   You book partial profits, say 50%, when the stock doubles. When the market dips, the remaining stock also falls back to your entry price. But this time, you've already secured gains on half your investment. You protected your profits and capital. And now, you can buy the stock again at a lower price.

Protecting profits in investing is like freezing or selling your gym membership. When the market is booming, sometimes

---

[57] Bull market is a period of generally rising stock prices and optimistic investor sentiment. In a bull market, investors expect further gains and buying is widespread. (Opposite of a bear market.)

[58] Bear market refers to a period of declining stock prices (typically a drop of 20% or more from recent highs) accompanied by widespread pessimism. In a bear market, investors often sell or avoid stocks, expecting further losses.

the smartest move is to secure your gains even if you're not actively growing your portfolio.

Because just like an unused gym membership, your profits can disappear if you do nothing. A sudden downturn can wipe out gains in an instant.

When the stock market booms, investors ride the wave of euphoria. But smart investors know better. They understand that money saved is money earned. Those who protect their profits emerge stronger market corrections, while others struggle to recover.

So, how do you protect profits without exiting the market entirely? You shift to safer bets. Here are a few examples of safer assets:

- **Low-beta assets:** These include bonds, GILT funds, and gold, which offer stability when the market is unpredictable
- **Defensive sectors:** These include healthcare, consumer staples, and utilities, i.e., sectors that remain stable even in turbulent times
- **Hedge your portfolio:** With put options on major indices or individual stocks, you can hedge against sudden price declines

Personally, I prefer GILT funds. These invest in government securities, carry low risk, and offer steady returns of around 6 to 7 percent. They're liquid too, so I can re-enter the market when valuations become attractive again. I like to say *"GILT mein jeene ka"* because when the market goes wild, I'd rather park safely than gamble with gains.

> **Myth Vs Reality**
>
> **Myth:** The only goal in the stock market is to make money
> **Reality:** Making money is half the game; the other half is protecting it. Without risk control, even big gains can vanish.

So whether it's your gym fees or your investment profits, don't let value slip away. Protect what you've earned, reposition wisely, and always remember — *a penny saved is a penny earned!*

FROM MY JOURNEY

Ever since the NIFTY crossed the 22,000 levels in March 2024, I've had a feeling of *déjà vu* and everything looks too good to be true. Everywhere I went, people shouted, *"The market will never crash!"* Twitter was flooded with sky-high price targets and my WhatsApp was full of messages like:

"Bro, the markets are on fire!"

"This time it's different! We are in a golden era!"

"Buy now or regret later!"

The problem with bull markets is that they make you feel invincible. You start thinking, *"Maybe this time it's different. Maybe the market really will really go up forever".*

Spoiler alert: it never does. Instead of riding the wave of euphoria to the end, I decided to act wisely. I stuck to my exit strategy, booking profits on majority of my portfolio, and moving the money into safer assets like GILT funds and gold ETFs.

I know what you're thinking, *"You sold majority of your portfolio? Isn't that extreme?"* Maybe. But I've been in the game long enough to know that trees don't grow to the sky. The higher the valuation, the more precarious the situation becomes. I'd rather protect my profits than chase more and risk losing everything in a crash.

I didn't want to be the guy who waits too long and then watches all their profits disappear like leaving dal makhani on the stove too long (and end up with a burnt disaster… you know the grief).

So, I shifted my profits to safer instruments. GILT funds didn't give me explosive returns, but they protected my capital and sometimes that's the biggest win of all.

Of course, the market didn't crash immediately. It continued to rise and a small part of me wondered if I had missed out. But as Warren Buffett says:

"Rule No. 1: Never lose money. Rule No. 2: Never forget Rule No. 1".

And that's exactly when the market began to wobble. In October 2024, the signs of a downturn were everywhere. The same people who were wildly bullish a few months ago started whispering about overvaluations, rising interest rates, and slowdowns.

Meanwhile, I sat comfortably. My capital protected, my profits secured, and my cash ready to deploy when the market finally corrected. Here's a snapshot of the comparative performance of NIFTY, GILTBEES, and GOLDBEES during that period:

Comparative performance of NIFTY vs GILTBEES vs GOLDBEES

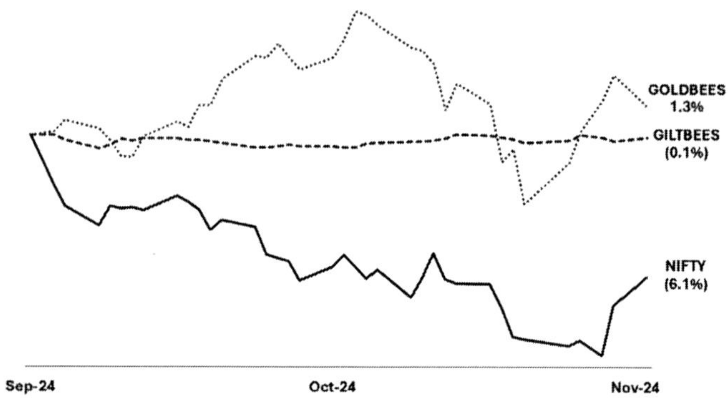

That night, I opened my diary and wrote down the lesson. Investing isn't just about how much you make; it's about how much you keep. Here's an excerpt from *My Investment Diary:*

My Investment Diary

Today, I learned that it is just as important to book profits as it is to make them. The market was rising, and it was tempting to stay fully invested. But instead of chasing further gains, I decided to lock in what I had already earned.

Now that the market is correcting, I see why that was the right decision. Protecting capital isn't about being cautious: it's about being smart.

Debit: "A lesson in capital preservation by shifting funds into safer assets at the right time"
Credit: "Capital preserved from market downturns"
(Net balance: A wise investor who understands that protecting capital is just as vital as growing it)

28 Oct 2024
(Monday)

THE BOTTOM LINE

There will always be ups and downs in the stock market. Bulls' storm, bears attack, and investors fluctuate between euphoria and panic. But if there's one golden rule that separates experienced investors from gamblers, it is this:

"It's not about how much you make; it's about how much you keep".

Chasing endless profits may feel exciting, but what good is a spectacular profit if you don't protect it from the next stock market crash? The biggest risk is not missing out on short-term gains but watching your portfolio crash.

So, if the markets are running too hot and everyone around you is making reckless bets, remember:

☑ Booking profits doesn't mean playing it safe; it means being smart

☑ Having some cash on hand doesn't mean missing out; it means preparing for the next big opportunity

When it comes to investing: *"Paise ka na jana bhi to aana hi hota hai!"* (A penny saved is a penny earned). So be smart, be disciplined, and make sure you aren't the last one standing when the music stops.

When prosperity comes, do not use all of it.

- Confucius
(Chinese philosopher)

26

THE SILVER BULLET

Have you ever felt overwhelmed by too many choices and wished for a one-click solution to simplify a complex problem?

I try to lead a reasonably healthy lifestyle, or at least I think I do. I try to eat clean, stay active, and make smart choices. But my deep, passionate love for food sometimes throws me off track.

Overall, I'm not obsessed with health metrics. My philosophy? If something is wrong, my body will sound the alarm. If I'm missing something important, surely my body will give me a clue, right?

I know I might sound like the uncle who refuses to go to the doctor unless he's on a stretcher. Not that I have anything against checkups; I just don't believe in having random tests done when there's no good reason for them. My logic is simple: "*Mah body, Mah rules!*" Yes, I know, I might be misusing that phrase, but there you have it.

My wife, on the other hand, is on a completely different level. She claims to be the health-conscious one in the house (yes, she says this while holding a large order of McDonald's fries in one hand and a burger in the other).

Recently, she decided to undergo a full-body diagnostic test to check her vitamin and mineral levels. I thought it was completely unnecessary until the results arrived.

It turned out that her vitamin deficiencies were longer than her shopping list. She was lacking vitamin D3, B1, B12, E, C, Iron, Copper, Magnesium, and several other elements I didn't even know humans needed to survive.

Panic spread and we went to the doctor. He took one look at the report and wrote us a prescription that was so long and complicated that I felt like I was managing a pharmaceutical warehouse. Iron tablets twice a day, vitamin B1 before breakfast, vitamin B12 before dinner, and vitamin D3 twice a week; the list just kept getting longer and longer. I was drowning in it.

At this point, I felt like Hrithik Roshan in *Zindagi Na Milegi Dobara;* not the cool, adventurous Hrithik, but the stressed-out stockbroker Hrithik. I kept an eye on the pill schedules, just as he kept an eye on the stock market numbers. Finally, frustrated, I asked the doctor, *"Isn't there a pill that works sensibly for everything?"*

His reaction was priceless. He gave me a slow, knowing smile, like the Joker in The Dark Knight after Batman slammed him down on the table. Then he said in a very matter-of-fact tone:

"Yes, just take this multivitamin twice a day. It covers everything reasonably well".

I was stunned. A single pill? A one-stop solution? Why didn't we start with this? I had spent a whole day looking at a hundred supplements, only to realize there was a shortcut. It was as if I had found a one-stop solution that fulfilled all needs.

MARKET LENS

Now, let's apply this multivitamin insight to the stock market. If you thought my wife's list of vitamin deficiencies was overwhelming, try analysing a company before you invest. It's chaos on another level. You have to keep an eye on sales growth, profit margins, valuation multiples, management quality, industry outlook, government policy, inflation trends, and even the state of the global economy. It's no less stressful than juggling multiple pills at different times of the day.

You might find yourself thinking, *"Isn't there one thing that can simplify all this?"*

Good news, it exists! I call it *"The Silver Bullet"*, or, in true Desi style, *"Ramban"*. What is this exactly?

Here's the trick: watch where *Private Equity*[59] (PE) firms or institutional investors are placing their bets. These firms have teams of analysts who spend months, sometimes years, analysing every financial detail before making a single investment. Their research covers financial health, market potential, competitive advantages, quality of management, risks, and future opportunities. In short, they do the heavy lifting for you. And since they invest millions (sometimes billions) of dollars, their due diligence is much more rigorous than that of a retail investor.

---

[59] Private Equity is investment capital provided by private investors or funds to acquire equity stakes in companies (often private companies or buyouts of public companies). PE firms invest large sums in businesses, aim to improve them, and later sell at a profit.

Following smart money is like taking a multivitamin instead of juggling a dozen pills. It's not a substitute for in-depth research, but it's a reasonable shortcut for those who don't have the time or expertise to analyze every stock in depth.

Institutional investors and PE firms can't afford to make reckless bets because their reputation (and a lot of money) is on the table. If you don't have the time to track all the financial data, it's wise to let the experts do the work for you.

Did You Know ?

Some of the biggest winners in the stock market, like Bajaj Finance and Divi's Labs, were backed by Private Equity firms before they became multibaggers. PE firms often recognise potential market leaders long before retail investors do.

FROM MY JOURNEY

My belief in this investment strategy comes from personal experience, not just theory. During my time at a Private Equity (PE) firm, I had a front-row seat to witness how meticulously these firms make investment decisions. Unlike retail investors, who often rely on gut instinct, media hype, or tips from acquaintances, PE firms follow a highly structured and disciplined process.

Each potential investment goes through multiple layers of research and vetting, starting from the junior analyst and moving up to the senior analyst, associate, principal, vice president, partner, and finally, the investment committee. At every stage, the process includes detailed financial modelling, market research, competitor analysis, and risk assessment. So, when a firm decides to invest, you can be sure that every angle has been examined, every number double-checked, and every scenario thoroughly stress-tested.

During my time at the PE firm, I became curious about how and where these firms invest. One firm made a significant investment in Himadri Specialty Chemical Limited, a company that had already caught my attention. At that stage of my investment journey, I hadn't yet developed the habit of conducting thorough research for my own portfolio. However, knowing how rigorously PE firms analyze their investments, I decided to follow their lead and bought shares in Himadri Specialty.

A few months later, the stock price nearly doubled. When the PE firm eventually announced their exit a few years later, I decided to sell my stocks as well and ended up receiving double my original investment. It was like applying the *Silver Bullet* strategy in real life; I was guided by the research from the big players, and it paid off. Here's an excerpt from *My Investment Diary:*

My Investment Diary

Today, I learned that following smart money can simplify investment decisions. Instead of trying to analyze every stock in detail, I can leverage the expertise of institutional investors who have already done the heavy lifting.

It's not about blindly copying them but about using their insights as a guide to identify high-quality opportunities.

Debit: "A lesson in identifying potential winners by tracking institutional investments"
Credit: "Profits gained from investing in Himadri Speciality"
(Net balance: A wiser investor who recognizes that following institutional moves can be a valuable shortcut to identifying strong investment opportunities)

10 Feb 2018
(Saturday)

This wasn't a one-off experience. I've used this approach several times since. When I don't have the time to scrutinise a potential stock, I look at where institutional investors are placing their bets. It's like having access to a free research team that spends months analysing opportunities, while I simply leverage their expertise.

That said, it's important to remember that institutional investors have access to resources, networks, and strategies that retail investors don't. Following their lead may give you an edge, but it's not a foolproof formula. Use it as a guide, not a guarantee.

Here's a list of key PE investments in India over the past few years, along with how these firms helped transform the companies:

Key PE Investments in India

Year	Company name	Private Equity	Stake	Key Outcomes (after 2 years)
2017	AU Small Finance Bank	TA Associates	-	Created India's largest small finance bank with over 10 million customers
2022	Yes Bank	Carlyle Group, Advent International	10%	Bolstered balance sheet and improved capital adequacy. Carlyle exited partially later
2017	Kalyan Jewellers	Warburg Pincus	-	Professionalize management, expansion into North India and franchise model launch
2015	Kolte-Patil Developers	KKR	-	Enabled financial closure, working capital support and debt reduction
2010	Himadri Speciality Chemicals	Bain Capital	25%	Strategic move into lithium-ion battery materials segment

THE BOTTOM LINE

If you lack the time, expertise, or patience to analyze every company on the stock market, don't worry; there's a shortcut. Just like a multivitamin simplifies your health routine, you can use PE firms and institutional investors to help you figure out where to invest. These firms take no chances. They do extensive research, analyze risks from all angles, and only back companies that pass their stringent filters.

However, this is not an excuse to turn off your critical thinking and blindly follow their moves. Just like taking a multi-vitamin doesn't mean you should eat junk food all day, following institutional investors doesn't grant you immunity from the need to scrutinize your investments thoughtfully.

So, the next time you feel overwhelmed by the complexities of stock picking, remember that there's a *"Silver Bullet"* for that. Follow the smart money, invest wisely, and let your portfolio benefit just as my wife did from her multivitamin!

It is far better to borrow wisdom than to borrow money.

- Benjamin Franklin
(American Polymath)

LOST BATTLES, WON WARS

What's harder — realising you've made a mistake or having the courage to admit it?

We all know the story of *The Emperor's New Clothes.* A fable so timeless that it continues to serve as a mirror of human nature. Let's revisit it together.

Once upon a time, there was an emperor who was obsessed with his looks and believed that looking powerful was as important as being powerful. Two cunning impostors arrived, claiming to have woven a magical fabric that was invisible to anyone who was incapable or hopelessly stupid. Eager to prove his intelligence, the emperor ordered the garment, even though he could not see it himself. His ministers, who were afraid of looking stupid, nodded, and pretended to admire the invisible masterpiece.

When the emperor finally "put on" his new robe and marched through the streets, his subjects praised him driven by the fear of being labelled foolish. But then, a voice rang out from the crowd, small but penetrating:

"But he's not wearing anything!"

A child, too young to understand the complexities of politics, spoke the truth. The illusion shattered. Rather than admitting his mistake, the emperor prioritized his pride above reality; what could have been a minor embarrassment became a legendary humiliation.

This tale is not just a fairy tale; it serves as a warning. Whether in business, investing, or life, many emperors live in their own illusions and refuse to admit mistakes until it is too late.

Take Paytm, for example. When UPI (Unified Payments Interface) was launched in India in 2016, it was a financial revolution enabling seamless, instant, and direct bank-to-bank transfers that made wallets redundant. But Paytm, which had built its empire on a wallet-based system, was hesitant to adapt. While competitors like PhonePe and Google Pay adopted UPI, Paytm stuck to its old model for too long, with cumbersome KYC processes for wallets in contrast to the frictionless UPI transactions.

Paytm's attachment to its wallet model was just like holding onto an old college hoodie — comfortable and nostalgic, but not exactly fit for a job interview (or, in this case, the future of payments). By the time Paytm fully transitioned to UPI, it had already lost its market supremacy.

Consider Nokia, once the undisputed king of mobile phones. The phrase *"Nokia wala phone"* was synonymous with durability. But as smartphones conquered the market, Nokia clung to its outdated Symbian operating system while Android and iOS took over. By the time Nokia finally adopted a new strategy with Windows Phone *(hello, Lumia!)*, the market had already shifted irreversibly. A company that had once dominated the mobile world had to sell its mobile division.

Whether it's an emperor or a business leader, the inability to accept mistakes and pivot quickly can turn a lost opportunity into a major defeat.

MARKET LENS

History teaches us that mistakes are inevitable, but refusing to acknowledge and learn from them leads to downfall. This lesson is particularly relevant in the stock market, where stubbornness can make the difference between recovery and total ruin.

Even the greatest investors have made mistakes. Warren Buffett openly admits that one of his biggest blunders was missing out on Microsoft and Google in their early years. He avoided Microsoft because he didn't fully understand the tech company model at the time (imagine being friends with Bill Gates and still not investing!). That decision cost him billions. But here's the key: Buffett didn't dwell on it. He accepted the mistake, learned from it, and moved on.

This mindset also applies to individual investors. They often hold on to loss-making stocks, hoping that one day they will recover. However, it's wise to cut your losses, reflect on what went wrong, and learn the lessons.

In the business world, the best companies recognize their mistakes quickly and pivot accordingly. Elon Musk once admitted that over-automating the production process at Tesla in 2018 was a mistake. He stated, *"Excessive automation at Tesla was a mistake. To be precise, my mistake. Humans are underrated"*. Instead of ignoring the problem, Musk adjusted and Tesla ultimately met its production goals. The conclusion? Admitting mistakes is a sign of wisdom.

Closer to home, Ratan Tata's decision to market the Tata Nano as "the world's cheapest car" backfired. The term "cheap" conveyed the impression of poor quality. Tata later admitted that this was a branding mistake. Tata Motors accepted the mistake, refocused on its strengths, and adjusted its approach.

If you admit to yourself that you have made a mistake, you can refocus, get rid of underperforming stocks, and seek better opportunities. Mistakes are part of the journey. The key is to recognize them and act on those insights.

Did You Know ?

Toyota once recalled over 1 crore cars due to safety defects, the largest recall in history. Instead of covering up the mistake, the company admitted it, fixed it, and came back stronger.

FROM MY JOURNEY

If Warren Buffett can admit his investment mistakes and Elon Musk can acknowledge his misjudgements, who am I to say I haven't made some terrible investment decisions too? Believe me, I've made many, none more painful than my penny stock disaster.

In my early days as an investor, I was lured by the promises of "multi-bagger" penny stocks. The logic seemed foolproof. If a stock jumps from ₹5 to ₹50, that means 10x returns! Intrigued by this seemingly magical math, I invested my money in different penny stocks.

Some stocks rallied and I felt like a stock market genius. *"I've cracked the investment code!"*, I thought. But then reality caught up. The stocks started to plummet. Instead of cutting my losses, I made the classic mistake; I doubled my stake. Believing they would recover; I continued to "average" (a classic strategy where investors keep buying more shares as the stock price falls, hoping it will eventually rebound). But they didn't.

What I failed to recognize were the red flags. Shaky financials, rising debt, and questionable management decisions. These weren't undervalued gems; they were *value traps*[60].

Worst of all was Rasoya Proteins. I truly believed Rasoya Proteins was a hidden gem. The company was in the edible oil business and with the rising demand for food in India, I thought it was a bull's eye. I jumped in with confidence and ignored the rumours of financial problems. At first, everything seemed fine. The stock price was stable and I was convinced I had picked a future multi-bagger.

But then the first cracks started to appear. The debts piled up, the quarterly results didn't add up, and something wasn't right. Nevertheless, I stuck with it. *"The markets are overreacting. It will recover"*, I told myself.

Spoiler alert: it didn't. Here's how the Rasoya Protein story unfolded over the next few years:

---

60 Value traps are stocks that appears cheap based on valuation metrics but continues to underperform due to fundamental weaknesses.

Rasoya Protein Stock Price Chart

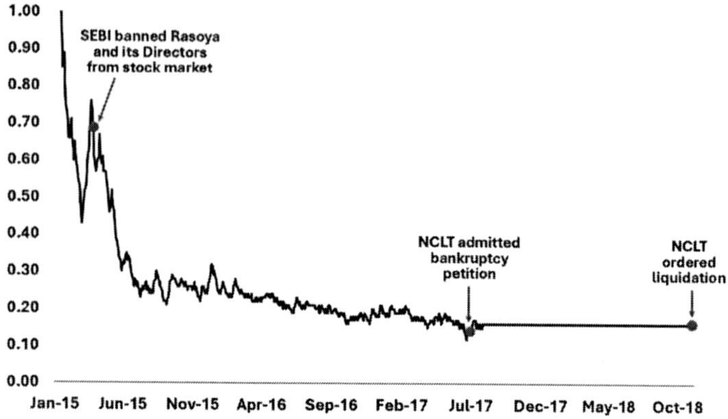

In 2017, Rasoya Proteins filed for bankruptcy and by 2018, the company was officially under liquidation process. My stocks? Completely worthless. I had ignored all the warning signs and held onto the stock until it was too late. Here's an excerpt from *My Investment Diary:*

My Investment Diary

Today, I learned that it is important to accept mistakes when investing. Holding onto a bad investment does not improve the situation; it just leads to greater losses.

The sooner you recognise a mistake and act, the better you can protect your capital and seize better opportunities.

Debit: "Significant losses by holding onto Rasoya Protein stocks instead of acknowledging the mistake early"
Credit: "An important lesson in recognizing missteps early and protecting capital"
(Net balance: A smart investor who understands that accepting small losses is the key to long-term financial success")

30 Oct 2018
(Tuesday)

The real reason I didn't sell. The *"sunk cost fallacy*[61]*"*. I had already invested so much money and time that I refused to admit my mistake. I kept telling myself, *"I've already come this far, I might as well wait"*.

It's like buying a movie ticket, realizing the movie is terrible, and still going to see it because you've already paid (we've all been there, right?).

---

[61] Sunk Cost Fallacy is a cognitive bias where someone continues an endeavour because of the resources (time, money, effort) already invested, rather than cutting their losses. In investing, this can lead to holding a losing stock because of the amount already paid, even when prospects for the stock are poor.

Wrong! The smart decision is to recognize a mistake and limit your losses. At some point, every investor faces a difficult decision — either admit a mistake or double down (and make it worse). Had I accepted reality and got out early, I could have saved a significant portion of my investment. Instead, I let hope cloud my judgment and watched my money evaporate into thin air.

THE BOTTOM LINE

As Warren Buffett wisely said, *"The most important thing to do when you find yourself in a hole is to stop digging"*. A bad stock pick, a missed opportunity, or holding on too long out of stubbornness, all of these can happen. What matters is how quickly you recognize, accept, and correct your mistakes.

Because here's the truth: the markets don't care about your ego. A stock won't rise just because you want it to, and denial won't undo a bad decision. The sooner you accept reality, the sooner you can move on, or at the very least, stop refreshing your portfolio hoping your stock will magically rebound.

Winning in the stock market isn't about being right all the time (otherwise we'd all be sitting on our personal yachts). It's about knowing when to pull back, regroup, and fight smarter.

So don't be like the emperor who walks around in invisible clothes, pretending everything is fine. Instead, be like the child who is not afraid to tell the truth, even if this truth is admitting, *"I was wrong"*. Sometimes the smartest thing you can do is to give up on a losing battle — because that's how you win the war.

The greatest mistake you can make in life is to be continually fearing you will make one.

- Elbert Hubbard
(American writer)

ART OF EXIT: 25-25-25 RULE

Have you ever done something and immediately wished you could rewind time, undo your actions, and make a different choice?

In the *Mahabharata*, the story of Abhimanyu is one of great valour, but with tragic consequences. As the son of Arjun, he was a skilled warrior, trained in advanced warfare. However, there was a fatal gap in his knowledge; he knew how to enter the *"Chakravyuh"* (a deadly military formation), but not how to exit it.

On the battlefield of Kurukshetra, when the Kauravas deployed the *"Chakravyuh"*, Abhimanyu saw his chance and charged in with confidence. He fought bravely, taking on warrior after warrior, but soon realised that he was surrounded and saw no way out. His father, Arjun, was too far away to lead him and his allies could not break through to help him. Despite his courage, he was outnumbered, trapped, and eventually killed.

Abhimanyu didn't fall for lack of courage or strength. He fought like a lion but walked into a trap with no way out. His story reminds us that even the bravest can be undone, not by the battle but by the absence of an escape.

Think that's just mythology? Take the U.S. withdrawal from Afghanistan in 2021. The decision to withdraw was made, but the implementation was chaotic and disastrous. The rushed, unplanned evacuation left thousands stranded, military facilities abandoned, and chaos reigned. The lack of a proper exit strategy not only cost the U.S. its reputation but also undermined its 20 years of effort.

Hence, knowing when and how to exit is just as important as knowing when to enter. In the end, winning isn't just about breaking in; it's about knowing when to get out before it's too late.

MARKET LENS

Let's talk about the stock market. If you invest without having an exit plan, you can land yourself in trouble. It's like getting on a bus without knowing your destination; you might arrive somewhere, but is it where you wanted to go?

My father has an interesting way of putting things. He says, *"Delhi ki bus pe chadhoge, Toh kabhi na kabhi Delhi pohnch jaoge"*, i.e., if you get on a bus to Delhi, you'll reach Delhi eventually. What he really means is simple. Your actions must align with your goals. If you're looking for quick profits, you shouldn't suddenly become a long-term investor just because your trade went wrong. And if you're a long-term investor, you shouldn't panic-sell at the first dip.

One of biggest traps I've seen is traders becoming investors overnight. This often happens when a trade goes wrong and instead of cutting their losses, the trader suddenly adopts a new philosophy, *"Paisa toh long run mein hi banta hai"* (money is always made in the long run). But wait, weren't you there for a short-term trade? Holding onto a losing position out of fear or ego is not a strategy; it's pure emotion.

Your exit strategy should be set before you even enter. You should know when to book profits, cut your losses, and adjust your strategy to market conditions. In the market, there's a difference between persistence and stubbornness. The smartest investors aren't just good at picking stocks; they also know when to exit.

When is it actually time to exit the market? There are several signs that suggest that the market is ripe for a downturn, i.e., stretched valuations, weaker GDP, increased market volatility, a tightening credit market, continued selling by FIIs, rising unemployment, lower government spending, and more.

FROM MY JOURNEY

Over the years, I have developed a rule of thumb for exits, which I call the 25-25-25 exit rule. It's simple and effective. When a stock reaches my price target (or what I think is fair value), I book 25% of my profit. If the stock rises another 10-15%, I book another 25%. If it rises further, I take another 25% off the table. The last 25% remains invested, just in case the stock has more room to run. I always keep 25% invested if there are no problems with the company's fundamentals or strategy.

Some may ask, *"Why not sell it all at once?"* The answer is simple. Momentum is real. Stocks that perform well often continue to rise, but I prefer not to rely on blind faith alone. By exiting gradually, I can take the upside with me while securing profits at the same time. I won't let greed or fear dictate my decisions.

As I write this in September 2024, the NIFTY has crossed the 26,000 level. To be honest, I think the market is overvalued. That's why I started booking profits when it reached 22,000. When the NIFTY hit 24,000, I sold another part of it. By the time NIFTY crossed 26,000, I had already booked 75% of my profits.

Myth Vs Reality

Myth: If I don't sell, I have lost nothing.
Reality: A loss on paper is still a real loss. A stock that falls by 50% must rise by 100% just to break even.

Now, before you think I'm hoarding cash like a dragon, let me clarify I have shifted my money into safer investments, such as GILT ETFs and gold ETFs. I have booked profits on 75% of my portfolio and reallocated to safer assets because it's not just about creating wealth; it's also about protecting it. I opened my diary and wrote down this lesson. Here's an excerpt from *My Investment Diary:*

My Investment Diary

Today, I learned that timing an exit is just as crucial as timing an entry. When the market rose, I didn't chase additional gains. Instead, I stuck to my exit strategy and secured profits step by step.

Now that the market looks overvalued, I realize how important this decision was; a profit is only real when it is booked.

Debit: "A lesson in strategic profit booking to protect profit and capital"
Credit: "Preserving capital and avoiding losses by exiting before market downturns"
(Net balance: A smart investor who knows that a timely exit is as important for long-term success as an entry)

25 Sep 2024
(Wednesday)

THE BOTTOM LINE

"Profit wahi jo haath mein aaye" i.e., only profit that counts is the one you take home. It's easy to get carried away by rising stock prices and see your portfolio grow on paper. However, the reality is that unrealized profits mean nothing until you book them. A clear exit strategy ensures that your gains don't disappear the moment the market turns against you.

Think of it like a Test match in cricket. You might be on a dream run, hitting boundaries left and right, but if you don't declare the innings at the right time, you risk ending up in a draw without reaching the finish line. It's not only about maximizing profits; it's about knowing when to book your profits before the game changes. Markets are unpredictable and even the best stocks don't rise indefinitely. A well-planned exit strategy allows you to lock in profits while leaving room for further upside.

Ultimately, the stock market rewards those who plan ahead. Even the boldest entry can end disastrously if you don't know the exit. So, like Abhimanyu in *"Chakravyuh"*, focus not just on getting in, but also on knowing how and when to get out.

The hardest thing in life is knowing which bridge to cross, and which to burn.

- David Russell
(Author of Last Dance)

29

PARAMPARA, PORTFOLIO, ANUSHASAN

Do you ever stop to rethink your decisions, or do you just stick to the original script no matter what?

Let me take you back to when I first met Brijesh, a fellow dreamer from my CA days, full of ambition and teenage confidence. At the age of 17, we thought we had our lives all figured out. The plan was crystal clear. Complete CPT (CA entrance) in one attempt, crack IPCC (CA Intermediate) by 18, pass the CA final exam by 21, and *voilà!* By 25, we would be successful professionals with comfortable jobs, sipping fancy *lattes* and living the dream. Pretty easy, right? But just like in Bollywood movies, life had a twist in store for us.

Initially, everything went as planned. We passed the CPT and breezed through the IPCC with ease, gearing up for the grand finale. However, when it came to the CA final, the script took an unexpected turn. I cleared it on my second attempt, but Brijesh, who was my sharp-as-a-tack friend, got stuck. *"Don't worry"*, I said, *"you'll make it next time"*. But the "next time" turned into five attempts and each failure hit him harder than an emotional climax in a Karan Johar movie.

I tried everything to cheer him up, including the classic "Maggi party" (a therapy for CA students in Delhi facing any failure). However, by the fifth attempt, it was clear that his CA journey resembled an *Ekta Kapoor* serial, going in vicious circles without any climax.

That was when I stepped in as a "wise elder" (read: overly opinionated friend) and urged him to make a fresh start. *"Why don't you switch to CFA?"* I suggested, hoping he would at least consider the idea instead of seeing it as a betrayal. After some convincing (okay, a lot of convincing), Brijesh eventually made the switch.

Fast forward a few years, Brijesh didn't just pass all three CFA levels; he aced them. Today, he's a successful wealth manager, thriving in an industry he never pictured himself in. When we catch up, we laugh about those CA days — the failed attempts, the late-night Maggi sessions, and the stubborn desire to stick to the original plan.

I remind him, *"You weren't stuck; you just needed a new script"* Because sometimes, life doesn't call for more persistence. It calls for perspective. Strength is not about holding on at all costs. It's about knowing when to let go and pivot.

And that is precisely the lesson. Life is not about stubbornly sticking to plan A. Sometimes, you need to take a step back, review your options, and change your plan. Because on the whole, nothing is set in stone (except, of course, my love of Maggi).

MARKET LENS

Many people come to me and ask, *"Bhai, bas ek stock bata do jo retirement tak hold kar sakein"* (Bro, just name a stock that I can hold until retirement). Sorry, folks! It's not 1990 anymore and Harshad Mehta is not offering personal tips over a cup of *chai.*

The reality is that "invest and forget" approach no longer works. You need to review and rebalance your portfolio, just like you adjust your playlist if you're tired of hearing *Baby Shark* repeatedly. Markets change, companies evolve, and even the strongest stocks can lose momentum. Every quarter, companies announce their earnings and stock prices react to this news faster than a *Bigg Boss* contestant picking a fight. If you don't keep an eye on your investments, you may wonder why your stock is falling faster than a bad Salman Khan movie on its opening weekend.

Markets are always evolving. A superstar stock from last year could be irrelevant today. A once-booming sector might now be struggling *(hello, IT stocks in 2020!).* If you don't track these changes, you could end up holding onto underperforming stocks while new opportunities pass you by, just like those *"I should have bought that stock"* moments we all regret.

Many investors pick a stock or mutual fund and then forget about it, treating their portfolio like an unattended pressure cooker. And what happens when you ignore a pressure cooker? It either whistles loudly with warning signals or, worse, it bursts.

Similarly, some stocks or mutual funds that once performed brilliantly may now be underperforming due to changes in management, strategy, or market conditions. If you don't review your investments, you may find yourself sitting on dead weight, expecting it to magically turn into gold.

Another key point to highlight is the importance of reviewing individual stocks as well as evaluating your overall portfolio. Market movements can distort your *asset allocation*[62] without you realising it, what was originally a balanced mix can drift into undesirable positions. Stocks that once made up 30% of your portfolio could now constitute 80%, exposing you to more risk. Without *rebalancing*[63], a single downturn could wipe out a significant portion of your wealth.

Let's talk about long-term investing. No, it's not about buying a stock and going into hibernation for the next 30 years. That's not how wealth is built. Long-term investing still needs regular check-ins. Here are a few rules to keep in mind:

☑ Book profits when a stock soars too high, because even the best stocks don't stay at the top forever.

☑ Accumulate more when a stock is undervalued. Think of it as "end of season sale" and focus on building your wealth.

Rebalancing is not about chasing returns. It's about managing risk, protecting gains, and ensuring your portfolio doesn't become a museum of past winners. The market will continue to evolve. The real question is, will your portfolio evolve with it?

---

62 Asset allocation is the strategy of dividing investments across various asset classes (e.g., stocks, bonds, real estate) to reduce risk and enhance returns.

63 Rebalancing is the process of realigning the weightings of assets in a portfolio to maintain the desired risk-return profile. Often involves selling outperforming assets and investing in underperforming ones.

FROM MY JOURNEY

Let me take you back to one of my earliest lessons in investing — straight from my father. Like many others, he was a staunch believer in long-term investing but without fully understanding its nuances. He assumed that if he just held onto stocks long enough, they would magically turn into multi-baggers.

It was year 2008 and his eyes set on Suzlon Energy. I'm pretty sure everyone has heard this story from the one uncle who lost a fortune in Suzlon and now hates the stock market as much as we hate pineapple on pizza. During the bull run leading up to the 2008 crash, my father invested a large sum in Suzlon at over ₹300, convinced that renewable energy was the future. To be fair, it still is, just not in our portfolios. However, he ignored the following warning signs, refusing to see what was coming:

- ☒ The company accumulated huge debt.
- ☒ The company missed earnings estimates.
- ☒ The company's implementation of a project was a mess.

Nevertheless, he held on to the stock and believed in its comeback. *"Accha stock hai, wapas uthega"* (it's a good stock, it will recover). Spoiler alert: It didn't.

By 2013, the stock had slumped to ₹5, cheaper than a *cutting chai*. When it finally recovered to ₹28 in 2014, he decided to sell, thinking it was the best he could get. At that time, it seemed like a wise decision, considering how low the stock price had fallen. But, in hindsight, the real mistake wasn't selling at ₹28; it was holding on for too long, like an old college hoodie that's two sizes tight, but still holds too many memories to let go.

Below is the stock price chart of Suzlon Energy from 2008 to 2016, illustrating its poor performance:

Suzlon Energy Stock Price Chart

Had he recognised the red flags earlier, he could have exited with a smaller loss and put the capital to better use. This experience taught me a valuable lesson. Conviction is powerful, but blind adherence is risky. A stock owes you nothing. If its fundamentals weaken, holding on in hope is rarely a winning strategy. It's better to move forward than to wait for a comeback that may never happen. I documented this lesson in *My Investment Diary*, a journal I started in 2015 to record my investment experiences. Here's an excerpt:

My Investment Diary

Today, I learned that neglecting rebalancing can lead to unnecessary losses. My father's experience with Suzlon Energy showed me that holding onto a bad investment out of hope only worsens the situation. Had he rebalanced earlier, he could have protected his capital and invested in better opportunities.

Regularly reviewing and rebalancing your portfolio is essential. If a stock's fundamentals weaken, it's wiser to cut losses and adjust before it's too late.

Debit: "The cost of holding onto a sinking investment"
Credit: "A lesson in preserving capital by knowing when to rebalance"
(Net balance: A smarter investor who understands that rebalancing is critical to long-term success)

06 Apr 2015
(Monday)

After this incident, I began following a structured review process. If a stock rises significantly, I gradually book some profits. If it falls, I check whether the fundamentals are still strong and if they are, I might even buy more. It's like cleaning out your closet; you don't keep wearing the same old shirts just because they looked great five years ago. You replace outdated pieces and make room for new ones. It's the same with stocks.

Myth Vs Reality

Myth: Long-term investing means never selling.
Reality: Smart investors don't just hold; they adapt. Long term isn't about ignoring signals, it's about evolving with the market.

THE BOTTOM LINE

Successful investing isn't about taking the right steps once and hoping for the best. It's about consistently reviewing, adjusting, and rebalancing, just like a DJ tweaks the mix to keep the party going. You book profits when the market is hot, accumulate when it cools down, and most importantly, adapt when the situation changes instead of stubbornly sticking to an outdated plan.

Rebalancing is not about chasing short-term trends or making impulsive movements. It's about aligning your portfolio with your long-term goals and ensuring that your investments continue to serve your overall financial objectives.

One of the biggest lessons I've learnt and something Brijesh would definitely agree with is that rigidity holds you back. Markets change, businesses evolve, and your portfolio should too. The stock market isn't a place for set-it-and-forget-it strategies. Review your investments regularly, make adjustments when needed, and evolve with the times while keeping your end goal in sight.

Think of the review process as a regular health check for your investments. Rebalancing your portfolio acts as a fitness program that helps eliminate unnecessary elements, strengthen the core, and keep your portfolio in shape. This should not just be a response to market fluctuations, but a necessary part of your financial journey.

Successful investing is not about reacting to every market fluctuation; it's about knowing when to take advantage of opportunities, when to make corrections, and when to move in a new direction. Review, realign, and repeat. Always in line with your long-term vision. That's the key to staying ahead in this game.

Finally, what could be a better investment philosophy than Amitabh Bachchan's famous line from the *Mohabbatein* movie — *"Parampara, Pratishtha (portfolio in our case), Anushasan".*

It is not the strongest of the species that survives, nor the most intelligent, but the one most responsive to change.

- Charles Darwin
(English naturalist)

30

SECOND OPINION, FIRST CHOICE

Would you rather make costly mistakes yourself, or learn from someone who's already been through them?

It was the summer of 2003, in my hometown Fazilka, Punjab. My uncle, a self-proclaimed DIY expert, had taken it upon himself to build his dream house, armed with nothing but a sketchpad, a pencil, and an abundance of overconfidence. Back then, in our small town, hiring an architect was a rarity. If you could draw a straight line, you were practically qualified to design a house. So, my uncle, full of enthusiasm, decided he didn't need any professional help. Who needs an architect when you've got graph paper and guts, right?

During my summer vacation, I watched him sketch his impressive "Kothi" (the Punjabi term for a large house), a 3000 square-foot masterpiece. It had everything. Three bedrooms, two living rooms, a couple of common rooms, a lavish kitchen, and a huge lobby. On paper, it looked like something out of a Bollywood movie and we were all genuinely impressed. But, my father, always cautious, suggested we must get the plans reviewed by a professional.

Initially, my uncle laughed off the idea. *"Why hire an architect when you can play 'Bob the Builder' yourself?"* he quipped. But after debates that dragged on longer than a Bollywood epic, he finally gave in and agreed to consult the one and only — *"Architect Sahb"*.

I honestly don't remember his real name because everyone just called him that. I expected the architect to shower my uncle with praise. Instead, he paused, frowned slightly, and ran his fingers over the plan like he had spotted a hidden flaw. Then, with a half-smile, he said, *"Ghar ta ban jauga, par saah nahi aana"* (The house will get built, but good luck catching your breath inside it).

It turned out my uncle had overlooked one crucial detail — *ventilation.* He had designed an architectural marvel, but he hadn't considered how people inside would get fresh air. To be fair, this wasn't entirely his fault. Homes in smaller towns were naturally airy back then, with open spaces and high ceilings. However, the design he created was a modern, enclosed structure where thoughtful planning was essential.

Ultimately, my uncle swallowed his pride and let the architect revise the design. That experience taught me an invaluable lesson about the importance of expertise and specialization. You may be skilled in many areas, but sometimes, you need a specialist. Seeking help isn't a sign of weakness; it's a smart decision.

This story serves as a reminder of the importance of having a trusted advisor, someone who brings experience, insight, and objectivity to the table. It's the difference between building a "house" and building a "house that's truly liveable". Even the brightest minds benefit from guidance.

A timeless lesson from the *Mahabharata* illustrates this perfectly. Arjun, the greatest warrior of his time, found himself paralyzed by doubt on the battlefield of Kurukshetra. Overwhelmed and torn, he couldn't decide his next move. Then Shri Krishna stepped in, not just as his charioteer but as his guide. Through the wisdom of the *Bhagavad Gita*, Krishna helped Arjun rise above his emotions and see clearly.

Now, imagine if Arjun had rejected Krishna's advice. He would have been like my uncle, armed with a grand plan but no real strategy. The right mentor doesn't just tell you what you want to hear; they tell you what you need to hear. They offer direction when uncertainty clouds your judgment.

The same logic applies to investing. Managing money requires specialized knowledge. Just as you wouldn't ask a general store owner for medical advice, you shouldn't rely on gut instinct or random stock tips to build wealth.

Whether you're constructing a "Kothi" or navigating your own Kurukshetra, one truth remains — *having a trusted advisor can make all the difference!*

MARKET LENS

Modern investing is more intricate than ever, requiring sharp insights and strategic decision-making. The days of simply buying a few blue-chip stocks, forgetting about them, and expecting them to turn into a fortune are long gone. Markets move in cycles, industries boom and bust, policies change overnight, and global factors influence local trends. Trying to navigate this chaos is like performing open heart surgery after watching a few YouTube tutorials; it might be possible, but not advisable.

Nevertheless, many investors believe that they do not need a second opinion. After making some gains in a bull market, they start to feel like the next Warren Buffett. But here's the thing. Bull markets often make everyone look like a genius. The real test of skill versus luck comes when the tide turns and markets correct.

So, why do people avoid seeking a second opinion? It often boils down to emotional biases. Investors often make decisions based on their "gut feeling" rather than logic. *"This stock just feels right"*, they say. But if feelings made money, we'd all be crorepatis by now.

Then there is confirmation bias, i.e., the tendency to seek out information that supports our existing beliefs. Investors often cling to positive news about their stocks while conveniently ignoring warning signs, as if they were re-watching a movie and convincing themselves that the ending wasn't so bad. The problem with this approach? The market doesn't care about your script; it follows its own.

Paytm's IPO is a prime example of emotional investing. People invested their savings into the IPO because they used and liked the app, forgetting that liking a product doesn't always mean it's a good investment. They ignored the warnings of overvaluation, let their emotions get the better of them, and watched their investments plummet. A professional advisor could have easily pointed out the red flags and helped them avoid this costly mistake.

Let's also talk about risk management. Many retail investors become reckless after their first profits, convinced they've *"cracked the market code"*. You might remember the story of Bill Hwang, a seasoned investor who lost $20 billion in just a few days. He placed oversized bets on a handful of stocks, believing he had everything under control. But the market had other plans. His downfall wasn't due to a lack of knowledge but to overconfidence and ignoring external advice.

Even the biggest names in the investment business world rely on a second opinion. Warren Buffett has Charlie Munger. Rakesh Jhunjhunwala had a team of trusted advisors. The best investors don't work in isolation; they have people who challenge their views, stress-test their investment theses, and ensure emotions don't cloud their judgment. An advisor can help you with diversification, risk control, tax optimization, and long-term planning. It's not always about finding the next multi-bagger; it's about ensuring your portfolio can withstand the test of time.

Myth Vs Reality

Myth: Advisors are only useful for the super-rich and HNIs.
Reality: A good advisor helps grow and protect wealth for all investors, including retail investors.

Over the years, I have noticed one thing. People are extremely hesitant to pay for financial advice. It's almost as if hiring an expert is seen as an unnecessary expense rather than a strategic investment. I often hear statements like, *"Why should I pay an investment advisor when I can do it myself?"* or *"I made great returns in the last year; why would I need help now?"*

And that's where the problem begins. Many investors don't realize that it's easy to make money during a bull market; the challenge lies in protecting those gains during a downturn. A skill that separates smart investors from overconfident ones. When your portfolio is small, mistakes may not feel as impactful, but as your portfolio grows, the stakes become higher. That's when a single wrong decision can undo years of progress.

I'm not saying that everyone should hire an advisor for every little decision. However, complexity increases as your assets grow. Think about it, when it comes to your health, you don't rely on Dr. Google; you consult a qualified doctor. The same logic applies to managing your wealth.

FROM MY JOURNEY

Let me share a story to illustrate this perfectly. I had a friend, let's call him "The Market Guru", who was convinced he had cracked the stock market. After making 30% returns during a bull market, he believed he was "*Rakesh Jhunjhunwala 2.0*". Every stock he picked seemed to be gold and every suggestion to seek a second opinion was dismissed with an *"Bhai, main samajhta hoon market"* (Market? Bro, I've got it all figured out).

It was almost comical, like the meme of the Nigerian actor, he held up his portfolio like it was a crown jewel and proclaimed, *"This is business!"* He believed that he dominated the market. His overconfidence was obvious. But as the saying goes, pride comes before a fall.

Then the market corrected. Some of the stocks he had blindly invested in, especially the penny stocks and high-risk bets, all crashed. One stock collapsed due to sudden changes in market direction, while another, a classic *pump-and-dump*[64] stock, lost 95% of its value in just a few months.

I still remember the day he called me. His voice had none of the confidence of a seasoned investor. Instead, he sounded just like Akshay Kumar in that famous meme: *"Mujhe toh chakkar aa rahe hain!"*

His problem wasn't a lack of knowledge; it was a failure to recognize what he didn't know. He had never considered risk management, diversification, or even basic asset allocation. A wealth advisor could have completely prevented this disaster. I documented this lesson in *My Investment Diary*. Here's an excerpt:

---

[64] Pump and dump is a stock manipulation scheme where operators hype up a thinly traded stock ("pump" it) to drive the price sharply up, then sell their holdings at the inflated price and exit ("dump" it), causing the stock to crash. Late investors are left with heavy losses.

My Investment Diary

Today I learned that getting a second opinion is not a weakness; it's a wise investment. Overconfidence can be dangerous, and ignoring the advice of an expert can cost much more than the fee of a good advisor. A fresh perspective can help identify risks, challenge preconceptions and protect my portfolio from costly mistakes.

Debit: "A valuable lesson on the importance of seeking expert advice to make better investment decisions"
Credit: "Losses avoided by avoiding high-risk pump-and-dump stocks"
(Net balance: A smart investor who knows that expert advice is not a cost, but a strategic investment in long-term success)

29 May 2018
(Tuesday)

Now, here's the tricky part: who qualifies as an expert? A fancy degree or a quick crash course in the stock market doesn't automatically make someone a smart advisor. Real-world investing goes beyond textbook knowledge. It's about managing risk, understanding market cycles, and knowing when to act.

This is where the greatest danger lies — *Finfluencers*. These days, anyone with a ring light and a bullish stock market chart can present themselves as a stock market guru. They promise shortcuts to success, claim to know "secret formulas", and lure thousands of investors into making blind decisions.

However, the truth is that many of them are not even legally authorised to give advice. In India, only SEBI-registered advisors are authorised to provide financial advice. SEBI enforces strict regulations to ensure investor protection, yet many retail investors skip this important check and trust viral content over verified expertise.

The most important lesson? If you are serious about building wealth, you should seek advice from a truly qualified advisor and always check that your advisor is registered with SEBI. A good advisor does more than just suggest stocks, but also helps you manage risk, navigate downturns, and protect wealth.

THE BOTTOM LINE

Managing money is like managing your health; you wouldn't rely on a WhatsApp forward for medical advice, so why would you trust your financial future to a random "expert"? As your portfolio grows, your strategy needs to mature with it. Professional advice is not an expense; it's insurance for your wealth.

A good advisor is like Shri Krishna on the battlefield; while you may have the skills of Arjun, without Shri Krishna's wisdom, even the sharpest arrow can miss its target.

In today's world of increasing specialization, investing is no different. Don't let emotions, overconfidence, or a flashy YouTube guru decide your financial future. When in doubt, seek advice from an expert, because in the unpredictable world of investing, it's not just about knowing what to do, but knowing who to ask.

To know the road ahead, ask those coming back.

- Chinese Proverb

CONCLUSION

Throughout this book, we've explored investing not as a rigid formula, but as a way of thinking and a mindset shaped by experience, reflection, and continuous learning. We've unpacked common mistakes, emotional pitfalls, decision-making biases, and the behavioural side of money. The aim was never to hand out fixed rules but to build a lens through which you can think more clearly, act more rationally, and invest more intentionally.

To wrap it up, I've grouped the key ideas into a memorable **J.A.L.F.R.E.Z.I.** structure. It's not an investing model or step-by-step approach, but a way to stitch together the core themes we've covered. While the book followed the natural journey of an investor, from foundational concepts to deeper strategies and eventually to exits, this final section rearranges those insights into thematic buckets. Think of it as a recap, reorganized for clarity and day-to-day relevance.

So, let's go through the **J.A.L.F.R.E.Z.I.** recipe:

JUDICIOUS START: BEGIN WITH CARE AND DUE DILIGENCE

"Soch Kar, Samajh Kar, Invest Kar"

"The *Golmaal* Theory"

"Success Starts with *No*"

"Think Beyond the Rearview"

Begin with scepticism. Avoid hype, question deeply, think ahead, and don't let past performance cloud your judgement. Sometimes, saying no is the smartest move.

ARTFUL ALLOCATION: MIX YOUR PORTFOLIO TO PERFECTION

"The 3-Plate Portfolio"

"The Dividend Delight"

Don't go all-in on a single flavour. Diversify across assets, balance wisely, and let each part play its role while dividends quietly do the heavy lifting.

LONG-TERM PERSPECTIVE: SLOW COOK FOR RICH RESULTS

"Decoding the 8th Wonder"

"Hold Right, Sit Tight"

"Aapda Me Avsar"

Think long term and stay the course. Let compounding do its work, ride through the market dips, and turn crises into opportunities.

FUNDAMENTALS FIRST: QUALITY INGREDIENTS ABOVE ALL

"Bhav Bhagwan Chhe"

"What Matters *Moat*"

"In Leaders We Trust"

Focus on substance, not shine. Bet on strong business models, trusted leaders, and fair valuations. Fundamentals always come first.

Rational Risk Management: Control the Heat and Don't Burn the Dish

"Risk Averse or Loss Averse?"

"Jack of All Trades"

"Lost Battles, Won Wars"

"Art of Exit: 25-25-25 Rule"

"Parampara, Portfolio, Anushasan"

Manage risk before chasing returns. Know your limits, follow a process, and have the discipline to exit when needed. Discipline is what keeps your portfolio alive.

Emotional Discipline: Mastering Greed and Fear

"The *Rapid* Formula"

"Tug of War: Greed vs. Fear"

"*N+1* Scenario"

"The *JOMO* Investor"

"Penny Saved = Penny Earned"

Keep emotions out of it. Stay calm in chaos, resist the urge to overdo, and remember that steady habits and small savings build serious wealth.

Zesty Innovation: Embrace New Flavours and Adapt to Change

"Go Global, Grow Global"

"The Next Big Bet"

"Good Debt, Bad Debt"

"*Double ka Meetha* Strategy"

"Ctrl + Alt + *Algo*"

Stay open to change. Explore global ideas, use smart debt, and adapt with evolving tools and strategies that keep your portfolio future-ready.

Individual Strategy: One Recipe Doesn't Fit All

"Mutual Fund Sahi Hai?"

"The Silver Bullet"

"Second Opinion, First Choice"

What works for others may not work for you. Know your goals, risk comfort, and time horizon. Your investments should fit you, not the crowd.

What Should You Do Now?

Dear reader, there is no final "tip" here. No magic formula. Just one final thought:

"The best investor is not the one who knows everything, but the one who keeps learning, questioning, and staying calm when others panic"

Refer to your investment diary. Learn from every mistake. Let go of the urge to predict and instead prepare.

Whether you're in your 20s investing your stipend, or in your 50s planning for retirement, the rules are the same:

Be curious. Be cautious. Be consistent.

Stock Jalfrezi was never just about giving stock tips. It was about building your own mental portfolio of stories, lessons and strategies.

And with that, it's time to close the book, but open the next chapter in your investing journey.

Invest with Trust!

AUTHOR'S CREDENTIALS

I'm Akashdeep Grover, a finance fanatic who has spent more time studying the stock market than anything else. As a Chartered Accountant (CA) and CFA Charterholder with over 10 years of experience, I've scrolled through more spreadsheets than Instagram feeds.

Most of my professional journey was with Ernst & Young (EY), where I worked on strategy and market research, helping companies solve complex financial puzzles.

But my story didn't start in a boardroom. I come from Fazilka, a small town near the India-Pakistan border, where life was slow, steady, and predictable. The biggest daily dilemma? Choosing between *lassi* and *chai.*

Then I moved to Delhi-Gurgaon, where every day felt like a stock chart — full of spikes, dips, and drama. For the record, the only "bull run" I saw in Fazilka was an actual buffalo chase, far easier to predict than most market rallies.

Now, I know what you're thinking. Punjabis and stocks? Not the most obvious combo. But let's change that perception. Punjabis have been hustling long before "entrepreneur" became a LinkedIn buzzword. We've rebuilt, innovated, and created legacies since Partition. Yet, when it comes to investing, it's usually our *Gujju* friends who take centre stage. And I say, *why should they have all the fun?*

So here I am, turning market chaos into clear insights. Join me on this journey of learning, unlearning, and wealth-building.